Ronald Harwood's plays include *The Dresser*, *Interpreters*, *Another Time*, and *Reflected Glory*. He is also the author of *Sir Donald Wolfit, CBE: His Life and Work in the Unfashionable Theatre*, and a history of the theatre, *All the World's a Stage*. He is the Editor of *The Faber Book of the Theatre*. He was visitor in Theatre at Balliol College, Oxford, was President of English PEN from 1990 to 1993, and has been President of International PEN since 1993.

TAKING SIDES

Ronald Harwood

faber and faber
LONDON · BOSTON

First published in 1995 in *Ronald Harwood: Plays 2*
This revised and updated edition first published in 1995
by Faber and Faber Limited
3 Queen Square
London WC1N 3AU

Photoset by Parker Typesetting Service, Leicester
Printed in England by Clays Ltd, St Ives plc

A CIP record is available from the British Library
ISBN 0–571–17772–7

2 4 6 8 10 9 7 5 3 1

For
Bernard Levin

Wilhelm Furtwängler (1886–1954) was the outstanding conductor of his generation, rivalled only by Arturo Toscanini. He was at the height of his powers when Adolf Hitler became Chancellor of Germany in 1933. Many of his colleagues, because they were Jews, were forced to leave; others, non-Jews, opponents of the regime, chose exile as an act of protest. Furtwängler decided to stay; as a result he was accused of serving Nazism. This was and still is the principal accusation made against him.

He came before a Denazification Tribunal in Berlin in 1946 which was conducted by his fellow Germans who questioned him for two days. He was cleared of all charges but was never able to cleanse himself entirely of the Nazi stench that still clings to his memory.

The Tribunal's evidence had been prepared in the first instance by the British, then taken over, apparently, by two groups of Americans: one, in Wiesbaden, which assisted Furtwängler with his defence; the other, in Berlin, which was responsible for building the case against him.

Little or nothing is known of the motives and methods of this second group which is the focus of *Taking Sides*. What is undeniable, however, is that Furtwängler was humiliated, relentlessly pursued and, after his acquittal, disinformation concerning him appeared in American newspapers. This may or may not have been justified. It all depends on the side you take.

CHARACTERS

MAJOR STEVE ARNOLD
EMMI STRAUBE
TAMARA SACHS
HELMUTH RODE
LIEUTENANT DAVID WILLS
WILHELM FURTWÄNGLER

The action takes place in Major Arnold's office
in the American Zone of occupied Berlin, 1946.

ACT ONE
February. Morning.

ACT TWO
Scene One: April. Night.
Scene Two: July. Morning.

SET

Major Arnold's office is an island surrounded by the rubble of a city flattened by Allied bombs. The room is in a former government building. Not everyone visiting the office need pass through the rubble. The office may also be reached from unseen approaches. The room is barely furnished but, incongruously, there is an ornate desk which Arnold uses. His German secretary, Emmi Straube, has a table, a typewriter and a field telephone. There are two other smaller tables; one with a record player and a pile of records, the other with an extension to the field telephone.

Between Arnold's desk and Emmi's table stands a plain upright chair which is for those being questioned. Nearer Arnold's desk there is a rather more comfortable chair for visitors. There is a door that leads to a waiting room.

In Act Two, central heating radiators are in place and the telephone system has been streamlined.

Taking Sides was first performed at the Minerva Theatre, Chichester, on 18 May 1995 with the following cast:

MAJOR STEVE ARNOLD	Michael Pennington
EMMI STRAUBE	Geno Lechner
TAMARA SACHS	Suzanne Bertish
HELMUTH RODE	Gawn Grainger
LIEUTENANT DAVID WILLS	Christopher Simon
WILHELM FURTWÄNGLER	Daniel Massey
Directed by	Harold Pinter
Lighting by	Mick Hughes
Costumes by	Tom Rand
Designer	Eileen Diss

The play (under the title *Za I Przeciw*) was performed on the same day in Poland at the Teatr im. Juliusza Slowackiego W. Krakowie with the following cast:

MAJOR STEVE ARNOLD	Marcin Kusminski
EMMI STRAUBE	Joanna Jankowska
TAMARA SACHS	Urszula Popiel
HELMUTH RODE	Mariusz Wojciechowski
PORUCZNIK DAVID WILLS	Marek Sawicki
WILHELM FURTWÄNGLER	Michal Pawlicki
Directed by	Tomasz Zygadio
Translator	Michal Ronikier
Designer	Jerzy Rudski

The play was presented with the same cast at the Criterion Theatre, London, on 3 July 1995 by Duncan C. Weldon in association with Criterion Productions plc, a Chichester Festival Theatre Production.

ACT ONE

February. Just before 9 a.m. Freezing cold. One miserable wood-burning stove. All wear overcoats, gloves, scarves. From the gramophone in Major Steven Arnold's office comes the sound of the last minutes of the final movement of Beethoven's Fifth Symphony, conducted by Wilhelm Furtwängler. ARNOLD is asleep, his legs stretched out on his desk. He could be any age, between thirty-five and early fifties.

EMMI STRAUBE is at her table listening to the music and watching ARNOLD. She is in her early twenties, pale, almost nondescript. In the bomb rubble, heavily wrapped up, like a vagrant, sits TAMARA SACHS, thirty-two, waiting.

HELMUTH RODE, late forties, wearing threadbare clothes and a Balaclava, enters the bomb-site. He starts rummaging for anything he can find. Then he hears the music but cannot identify its source.

LIEUTENANT DAVID WILLS, aged twenty-four, enters purposefully through the bomb rubble. RODE scuttles away. DAVID passes and disappears around the back of the office. TAMARA barely glances at him.

The music continues. ARNOLD sleeps. EMMI listens and watches. The office door opens and DAVID reappears. He sees ARNOLD asleep and retreats. After a moment, the music ends and EMMI takes off the record.

EMMI: Major Arnold, the music has ended.
    (*He doesn't stir.*)
    Major Arnold?
    (*He wakes with a start, as if from a bad dream.*)
    The music has ended, Major.
    (*He breathes more easily.*)
ARNOLD: I wish you'd call me Steve, Emmi.
EMMI: You fell asleep.
ARNOLD: That's true, Emmi, I did.
EMMI: It is very difficult for me to understand how you can fall asleep during Beethoven's Fifth Symphony.
ARNOLD: Then I'll explain, Emmi. I fell asleep during

I

Beethoven's Fifth Symphony because Beethoven's Fifth Symphony bores me shitless.

EMMI: You are joking again. Are you joking? I am never sure when you are joking. I think you are always joking when you are being coarse.

ARNOLD: No, Emmi, I am never joking when I'm being coarse.

EMMI: I don't like it when you are coarse.

ARNOLD: Then you must be having a really bad time of it, Emmi.

EMMI: You should listen to Beethoven carefully, Major. My favourite is the Eighth Symphony. But you should listen especially to the Ninth. Beethoven wrote it in his last years. It is one of the most beautiful pieces of music ever written. You should listen to it, Major.

ARNOLD: Is it the same length as Number Five? Or as he got older did he write shorter?

EMMI: Yes, you are joking, but you must listen to it, Major. That's why I have brought these recordings so that you should know with whom you are dealing.

ARNOLD: I know with whom I'm dealing. (*He goes to the stove, warms himself.*) I knew another band leader once. Name of Dix Dixon. Small time. Alto sax. Not bad. Not good, but not bad. Played one night stands in Illinois and Michigan. A house he owned, where he and the band used to stay, burned down. Lost everything. Well, almost everything. But I got him. You know how? Because there's always one question the guilty can't answer. Get a sign writer, write it big: THERE'S ALWAYS ONE QUESTION THE GUILTY CAN'T ANSWER. In Dix's case, it was, 'How come, Dix, everybody lost everything except you? You've got your clothes, your sax, how come?' Couldn't answer. He was dumb. Boy, was he dumb. Owed the bookies. You understand, don't you, Emmi? He burned down his own house for the insurance money. We used to call that Jewish lightning.

(*He chuckles; no response from* EMMI.)

How many people do I have to see before the big boy's due?

EMMI: (*Consulting a file*) Just one. Helmuth Rode. Second violinist, 1935 to the present. Also, there is a request from

2

Wiesbaden that you see a Mrs Tamara Sachs. I have talked
to her on the telephone and she will be coming at two
o'clock.

ARNOLD: Anything from Wiesbaden's got to be bad news.
What's this Mrs Sachs want?

EMMI: She wouldn't say. Oh, and, Major, a young officer put
his head round the door a moment ago, saw that you were
asleep and then disappeared.

ARNOLD: Who was he?

EMMI: I don't know. I have never seen him before. (*Consulting a
message pad.*) And two other messages. Captain Vernay may
visit later. Colonel Volkov will not be attending.

ARNOLD: That's a relief. Nothing from the British?

EMMI: No.

ARNOLD: Where's that young officer now?

EMMI: I don't know, he came and went.

ARNOLD: Go find him, will you, Emmi?

(EMMI *exits.* ARNOLD *adds wood to the heater. In the rubble,*
RODE *re-appears, crosses the bomb-site, stops to pick up a
cigarette butt and then hurries off towards the rear of* ARNOLD's
office and disappears. TAMARA *sits and waits.* EMMI *re-enters,*
holding the door for DAVID *who comes to attention, salutes*
smartly.)

DAVID: Lieutenant Wills reporting to Major Arnold. Sir.

ARNOLD: For Chrissakes I hate that shit, cut it out. My name's
Steve. What's yours?

DAVID: (*Slightly disconcerted*) David. David Wills.

ARNOLD: Who are you?

DAVID: I've taken over from Captain Greenwood. I'm your new
liaison officer with Allied Intelligence.

ARNOLD: What happened to Hank?

DAVID: Captain Greenwood was ordered to Nürnberg. Seems
they need more interpreters at the trial.

ARNOLD: So you're dealing with the British now.

DAVID: Yes, sir.

ARNOLD: You call me sir again, I'll make you listen to
Beethoven.

(DAVID *only half smiles.*)

3

You seen that Limey major yet, the one who talks like he's got ice cubes in his mouth? I can't tell if he's speaking German or English, what the hell's his name?

DAVID: Major Richards.

ARNOLD: Yeah, Alan Richards.

DAVID: I talked to him this morning but he was just rushing off to an urgent meeting.

ARNOLD: An urgent meeting. Yeah, the Hinkel Archive.

DAVID: Yes.

ARNOLD: Do you know what's in the Hinkel Archive?

DAVID: No.

ARNOLD: And if it turns out to be important, you think the British are going to share it with their allies?

DAVID: He said he'd call to let you know. He said he was very disappointed. He wanted to be here today. Especially today.

(ARNOLD *eyes him up and down.*)

ARNOLD: We recruiting children now?

DAVID: (*A smile*) I guess so.

ARNOLD: Where you from?

DAVID: I was born here.

(ARNOLD *smiles, waits, gives no help.*)

Not in Berlin. In Hamburg.

(*Still no help from* ARNOLD.)

I escaped in '34. When I was twelve.

(*Pause.*)

My parents sent me to my uncle in Philadelphia. They were to follow. But they delayed and delayed. They did not follow.

(*Nothing from* ARNOLD.)

Our family name is Weill. But that doesn't sound well in English. My uncle changed it to Wills.

ARNOLD: Did you hear that, Emmi? David here was born in Hamburg.

EMMI: Yes, I heard.

ARNOLD: I'm sorry about your parents.

(*Uneasy pause.*)

Oh, this is Emmi Straube. She records the interviews. She's

4

been with me a week. She's a good German, aren't you, Emmi? Her father was in the plot against Adolf.
(*Pause.*)
Well, what kind of an intelligence officer are you, David? You should have asked a question. You should have asked, 'But how do we know she didn't report her father for being in the plot against Adolf?' Isn't that what he should've asked, Emmi?
(*No response.*)
Emmi's okay. We've checked her out. You're okay, aren't you, Emmi?

EMMI: Shall I see if Mr Rode is here? It's after nine.

ARNOLD: When I say so, Emmi, when I say so. (*To* DAVID.) I like to keep them waiting. Makes them sweat. Which is a kindness in this weather, wouldn't you say?

EMMI: I expect Mr Rode's here, Major.

ARNOLD: She won't call me Steve, David. She is so correct. And she likes books and poetry and she's just crazy for Beethoven, aren't you, Emmi? Do you like Beethoven, David?

DAVID: Yes.

ARNOLD: Yes. I thought you looked funny when I threatened you with the old bastard. And I guess you admire musicians.

DAVID: Some.

ARNOLD: Don't.

DAVID: Don't what?

ARNOLD: This is like a criminal investigation, David. Musicians, morticians, lawyers, butchers, doctors, clerks. They're all the same. I saw Bergen-Belsen two days after it was liberated. I know what I'm talking about. I've seen things with these eyes – do you know what I'm talking about, David?

DAVID: Yes.

ARNOLD: Think of your parents. Don't think of musicians. We're after the big guy here, the band leader, that's the one we're going to nail. You know what I call him, David? I call him a piece of shit. I call 'em all pieces of shit.

5

DAVID: Captain Greenwood said hard evidence against him is difficult to come by.

ARNOLD: Let's talk about it after we get through with this guy Rode. Here's how we do it. This is my show, I ask the questions. If you want to ask a question, raise a finger so he can't see. I'll signal yea or nay. Understood?

DAVID: Yes.

ARNOLD: I'll explain my technique. I tell the shitheads why they're here. Then I only ever ask two questions. First, anything that comes to mind. 'How you feeling today?', 'Are you getting enough to eat?', 'You need some cigarettes?' Real friendly. Second, I say, 'I see from your questionnaire that you were never a member of the Party, is that right?' 'Absolutely right, I was never a member of the Party.' And then I wait. I say nothing. I wait. And then they talk. Oh, boy, do they talk. And they'll tell you what a great guy the band leader is, how he defied Adolf and Hermann and Josef. Oh yes, and they always get in the baton story.

DAVID: What's the baton story?

ARNOLD: How many have I questioned, Emmi?

EMMI: Twenty-eight.

ARNOLD: So this guy?

EMMI: Helmuth Rode –

ARNOLD: Rode, he'll be the twenty-ninth. You'll hear the baton story for the first time, I'm going to hear it for the twenty-ninth. Oh yeah, and they always manage to find out Emmi's last name, don't they, Emmi? Straube, they say. Any relation to Joachim Straube? My father, Emmi says. A great man, they say, a great hero. You see, David, what they're trying to do is cover the band leader in roses in the hope they'll come up smelling just as sweet. But it's difficult to smell sweet after you've crawled through raw sewage. I was in insurance before the war, a claims assessor, what were you in?

DAVID: College.

ARNOLD: And when all this is over?

DAVID: I'd like to teach history.

6

ARNOLD: History. You need a good memory for history, don't
you? All those dates and battles. Your memory good?

DAVID: Not bad –

ARNOLD: Me, I've got a terrific memory. I've been examined
by psychologists. Because of my memory, nothing else.
I've got what they call 'total recall'. I remember
everything. It's a curse. (*Suddenly as if briefly invaded by a
memory which he shakes off.*) Yeah, a curse, believe me.
But I'm bad at names. It's what the shrinks call 'selective'.
Tell you the truth, my recall's not total, but it's pretty
good. Yeah, insurance. I was trained by a guy called Lou
O'Donnell, a kind of Jimmy Cagney type. Pushy, smart,
persistent, boy, was that guy persistent. Lou taught me to
look out for what he called 'repetitive evidence', because
ninety-nine times out of a hundred it covers a conspiracy
to defraud. You think a whole orchestra, what, a hundred
and twenty or so guys, could be orchestrated?

DAVID: I don't know, I guess it's possible –

ARNOLD: Yeah, me too, I guess it's possible. Okay, Emmi,
let's get Mr Rode in.

(EMMI *exits.*)

You sit there.

(DAVID *sits and* ARNOLD *goes to his desk.*)

Remember, I do the talking. Just the two questions, then
we wait. You'll see.

(EMMI *re-enters.*)

EMMI: Mr Helmuth Rode.

(RODE *enters, removes his Balaclava, bows to* ARNOLD *and*
DAVID. EMMI *sits at her table and takes notes.* RODE *glances
nervously round, twists his neck to read the record labels.*)

ARNOLD: Sit down, Helmuth.

(RODE *sits;* ARNOLD *consults a file.*)

I want you to understand why you're here. This is a
preliminary investigation into Wilhelm Furtwängler,
former Prussian Privy Councillor, who is banned from
public life under Control Council Directive No. 24 and
who's applied to come before the Tribunal of Artists of the
Denazification Commission. We're interested in what he

7

was up to from 1933 to the end of the war, understood?

RODE: Yes.

ARNOLD: I have your questionnaire here. (*Reading.*) Helmuth
Alfred Rode. Second violinist, Berlin Philharmonic
Orchestra since 1935. What's it mean, second violinist,
Helmuth?

RODE: It means I wasn't good enough to be a first violinist.

(*He chuckles, looks round for approval;* ARNOLD *grins
encouragingly.*)

Mind you, you have to be pretty good just to be a second
violinist in the Berlin Philharmonic. Even though I say so
myself.

ARNOLD: And according to your questionnaire, Helmuth, you
never joined the Party.

RODE: Me? Never. Never.

(*Long silence;* ARNOLD *just watches him and waits.*)

I hated them. Believe me, please, I know everyone says now
they were never Nazis, but in my case it is absolutely one
hundred per cent true. I am a Catholic, a convert, it would
have been totally against my conscience.

(*Silence.*)

It's difficult to explain what it was like. Terror, that's what
you felt from morning till night, even asleep, you felt terror.

(*Brief silence.*)

In the early days, of course, we were much more open in
opposition. I'm talking about '33, '34. When I think back on
the things I said, I shudder. My God, I used to tell jokes,
anti-Hitler jokes, I was well known for my anti-Hitler jokes.
For example, this joke, it was very famous around '33, '34. A
couple of old Jews. One says to the other, 'I have two bits of
news for you, one good, one bad.' 'Tell me the good news
first.' 'Hitler's dead.' 'And the bad news?' 'It isn't true.'

(*He chuckles; looks round; nothing from the others.*)

That's the sort of joke I used to tell.

(*Silence; he wipes sweat from his brow.*)

You want to know about Dr Furtwängler? This man is
without doubt one of the most courageous people it has been
my honour to know. We all acknowledge he is a god among

musicians. In my humble, second violinist opinion, the
greatest conductor alive. True, I have not played under
Arturo Toscanini but I have heard his recordings, and the
emotion is not the same. Toscanini is a metronome. Dr
Furtwängler is an artist. No, no. Wilhelm Furtwängler is
unquestionably a genius, without equal.
(*Silence; he loosens his coat, wipes his brow again.*)
Is it true you're going to interview him today?
(*Silence.*)
Berlin is so full of rumours. I heard –
(*Silence; smiles.*)
You hear things all the time. If rumours were edible we'd all
be well fed. If I may say so, I hope you see to it that he's
properly guarded. There are so many crazy people about.
(*Silence.*)
He gave comfort in terrible times, what man can do more?
(*Silence.*)
Here's something that may interest you. On a famous
occasion, I think it was the second Winter Assistance charity
programme, an all Beethoven concert, this was in '35, it was
suddenly announced that Hitler himself was going to attend.
Well, you can imagine, the Maestro was outraged. You know
how angry he was? He ripped the wooden covering off the
radiator in his dressing room, that's how angry he was.
Because what could he do? He couldn't tell Hitler not to
attend.
(*Chuckles, looks round, silence.*)
You see, the problem was the Nazi salute. He absolutely
refused to give it. Now this I heard him say with my own
ears, I heard him say, 'I don't have to acknowledge him at
all,' over and over again, I heard him say that. But how could
he avoid giving the Devil's salute with Satan actually present
in the audience? You know who came up with a solution?
(*Modestly taps his chest with his thumb.*) I said, 'Maestro, why
not enter with your baton in your right hand? Hitler will be
sitting in the front row. If you give the salute with the baton
in your hand, it'll look like you're going to poke his eyes
out.' (*Chuckles.*) He was really grateful to me for that

9

suggestion. He came on to the podium, baton in his right hand which meant he couldn't give the salute. He just bowed quickly, turned immediately to us, and even while the audience was still applauding he gave the signal to begin. (*Smiles fondly at the memory*.) I tell you in confidence, after the concert, I did something disreputable. I stole that baton. As a memento of a great act of courage. I still have it. I should have brought it to show you.

(*Silence*.)

Mind you, it was always a joke in the orchestra. The Maestro's baton. He has a very eccentric technique. (*Stands and demonstrates*.) He waves, he sways, he jiggles. God knows when you're meant to come in. His downbeat was always the subject of jokes. Other musicians used to ask us, how do you know when to play the first chord of the 'Eroica'? When his baton reaches the third stud on his shirt, we'd say. Or, how do you know when to start the semiquavers at the beginning of the Ninth? We used to tell them, the moment the Maestro enters, we all walk round our chairs three times, sit down, count to ten and play. Or. When we lose patience. (*Chuckles, sits again; silence*.) Yet he can produce musical sounds like no other human being alive. (*To* EMMI.) I hope I'm not going too fast for you, Fräulein – ?

EMMI: Straube.

RODE: Straube. Any relation to Colonel Joachim Straube?

EMMI: My father.

(RODE *rises*.)

RODE: I am deeply honoured to be in your presence, Fräulein Straube. Your father was a true patriot. A man of God. *Requiescat in pacem*. (*He crosses himself; sits; silence*.) No, no, I want to say categorically that Wilhelm Furtwängler did not serve the regime. None of us who were members of his orchestra served the regime. Forgive me if I make a philosophical observation, but Wilhelm Furtwängler is a symbol to the entire world of all that is great in culture and music and the Nazis needed him. They needed him to make themselves respectable.

(*Silence*.)

(DAVID *raises a discreet finger.*)

ARNOLD: You have a question for Helmuth, David?

DAVID: Yes. There's a photograph, isn't there, Mr Rode, of Dr Furtwängler shaking hands with Hitler. How do you explain that?

RODE: But that's the concert I was talking about, the all Beethoven programme, when he came on with his baton in his right hand to avoid giving the salute. As I said, Hitler was in the front row and at the end of the concert, he suddenly stood up, went to the platform and offered the Maestro his hand. And the Maestro took it, what else could he do? That's all there was to it. I was there. I witnessed it. It was probably a calculated act, not spontaneous at all, because they wanted the Maestro on their side, of course they did, and so they had photographers there, and what could the Maestro do, he simply had to shake Satan's hand? That's all there is to it.

(DAVID *is about to ask another question but* ARNOLD *signals him to wait.*)

And he did not conduct *Die Meistersinger* at the Party Congress in Nürnberg in 1935. We played it the evening *before* the Congress. The music was quite separate from the politics. That is the Maestro's creed: politics and art must be kept separate. It's the same with the Devil's birthday. It was the evening before, 19th April, not the 20th. And the Maestro was tricked into it. Usually, when they wanted him to conduct on such occasions, he managed to get his doctors to diagnose spondylitis – inflammation of the vertebrae in the back and neck, common in conductors, and very, very painful. But for Satan's birthday in 1942, Goebbels got to the doctors first and that was that. (*Brief pause.*) And don't forget, please, the Maestro had to flee to Switzerland only last year, just before the war ended, because he learned that the Gestapo were about to arrest him. This is an honest, good man we are talking about. And the greatest conductor alive.

(*Again* DAVID *raises a finger.* ARNOLD *nods.*)

DAVID: Mr Rode, you only joined the Berlin Philharmonic in 1935. Where were you before that?

RODE: I was a member of another orchestra. In Mannheim. But in 1935, several vacancies arose in Berlin. I auditioned – (*Loses confidence. Becomes agitated.*) Yes, yes, but on the other hand Dr Furtwängler, personally, was very good to Jews. He helped a lot of Jews escape, Jews who were no longer allowed to be members of the orchestra, although he fought to retain them for as long as he could. His secretary, Berta Geissmar, was a Jewess. He relied so much on her. In the end, he had to help her to escape, too. She is now, I believe, in England, secretary to Sir Thomas Beecham. He's also a conductor but he is not Dr Furtwängler.

ARNOLD: Helmuth, do you know Hans Hinkel?

RODE: (*Alarmed*) Do I know Hans Hinkel?

ARNOLD: That's what I asked.

RODE: Do I know Hans Hinkel?

ARNOLD: You seem to understand the question, Helmuth, now how about answering it?

RODE: But how could I know such a man? Hans Hinkel was in the Ministry of Culture, how could I know such a man? (*Silence.*)

I hear he kept this archive, files, records – (*Fishing.*) Do you know what's in the archive, Major?

ARNOLD: I was just going to ask you that, Helmuth.

RODE: Me? How should I know what's in the archive? (*Silence.*)

The only thing I've heard is that there are letters from people swearing loyalty to the regime, that's all I know. (*Silence.*)

My personal, second violinist opinion, for what it's worth, is that Hinkel was in fact a very low level functionary, his archive won't have anything of interest. (*Silence.*)

ARNOLD: Okay, you can go now, Helmuth.

RODE: That's it?

ARNOLD: Get out, Helmuth.

(RODE *rises, bows to all three and goes to the double doors. As he opens them he stops dead, bows deeply to someone in the waiting room.*)

RODE: (*Awed*) Maestro!
    (EMMI *rises involuntarily as* RODE *exits, beaming, closing the door.*)
EMMI: (*Equally awed, going to the door*) He's here, Major –
ARNOLD: Sit down, Emmi.
    (*She sits.*)
    We're going to keep him waiting, too. (*To* DAVID.) So now you know the baton story, David.
DAVID: Yes, but Captain Greenwood is right. When it comes to hard evidence –
ARNOLD: (*Interrupting*) Get us some coffee, Emmi, will you? And, Emmi, don't offer coffee to the leader of the band. Don't even greet him, okay?
    (EMMI *goes.*)
    Jesus, when are they going to fix the central heating? My scrotum feels like a shrivelled prune. Probably looks like one, too.
    (RODE *hurries across the rubble.* TAMARA *stops him, questions him, then both disappear, quickly in opposite directions,* TAMARA, *like a fury, towards the office.* ARNOLD *adds wood to the stove.*)
    Let me tell you something, David, the evidence, hard or soft, doesn't matter, because I have the one question he's going to find it impossible to answer.
    (*A commotion in the waiting room. A woman's voice shouting.* ARNOLD *goes towards the door but* EMMI *comes rushing in, highly agitated.*)
EMMI: There's a woman attacking Dr Furtwängler.
    (TAMARA *bursts into the room like an avenging angel. She is prematurely grey, intense, driven.*)
TAMARA: This is an outrage, who's in charge, I have to see who's in charge –
    (*Overlapping, confused, and at speed.*)
ARNOLD: Get out of here, who the hell –
TAMARA: Have you any idea who's sitting out there – ? Wilhelm Furtwängler is sitting out there –
ARNOLD: Emmi, call the guard –
    (EMMI *makes for the door but* TAMARA *grabs* EMMI *and starts to shake her.*)

TAMARA: You're crazy, you're all crazy, you don't know what you're doing –

ARNOLD: David, get hold of her –

(DAVID *tries to grab her but she turns on him and starts pounding him with her fists.*)

TAMARA: You can't do this, you can't do this –

(*Just as suddenly she stops, tries to catch her breath, forlorn, distraite.* EMMI *tries not to whimper.*)

I'm sorry. When I saw him, I lost all control. Everything went out of my mind.

ARNOLD: Why don't you sit down for a moment, I'll call a medic –

TAMARA: No, no. I have to talk to you. Are you in charge?

ARNOLD: Who are you?

TAMARA: My name is Tamara Sachs.

ARNOLD: (*To* EMMI) Isn't this the one I'm seeing at two?

DAVID: Sit down, Miss Sachs.

TAMARA: Mrs Sachs.

DAVID: Emmi, get her a glass of water.

TAMARA: I have something of importance to tell you about Wilhelm Furtwängler.

(*Silence.*)

ARNOLD: Okay, Emmi, get us all some coffee.

DAVID: Please sit down, Mrs Sachs.

(TAMARA *sits.* EMMI *exits quickly.*)

TAMARA: I told them about it in Wiesbaden. They said I must tell you. Then I heard you were interviewing him today. I have material evidence to give.

(ARNOLD *considers for a moment.*)

ARNOLD: Okay. But just wait for my secretary to come back so she can take a record.

(*Silence.*)

TAMARA: You see, I am trying to find some proof that my husband, Walter Sachs, existed.

(*Silence.*)

Dr Furtwängler may be able to provide that proof. I've been waiting since the early hours. Then, when I actually saw him – (*She is lost for a moment.*) Could he come in, please?

ARNOLD: No, he can't come in.

DAVID: Was your husband a friend of his?

TAMARA: No. My husband, Walter Sachs, was the most promising young pianist of his generation.

DAVID: Were they colleagues, perhaps?

TAMARA: No. That's just the point.

(EMMI *returns with a tray of coffee and cups, flustered but pleased, a little excited.*)

EMMI: Dr Furtwängler spoke to me. He wants to know how long he is to be kept waiting.

ARNOLD: Emmi, put the coffee down, then go out there and tell him in these words, these exact words, mind, tell him, 'You'll wait until Major Arnold's ready to see you or until hell freezes over, whichever takes longer.' You got that, Emmi? And don't say anything else, okay?

TAMARA: Can't he come in, please?

ARNOLD: Go on, Emmi. Then come back and take notes. I'll do the coffee.

(EMMI *goes out.*)

Tamara, how do you take your coffee?

TAMARA: Is there cream and sugar?

ARNOLD: There is in the American Zone.

(*He serves her coffee;* EMMI *returns, sits at her table.*)

Okay, Tamara, let's hear what you have to say. You handle this, David. You and Tamara seem to have a certain – rapport. I'll just sit here and listen.

DAVID: Whatever you say, Mrs Sachs, will be treated as confidential.

TAMARA: But I don't want it treated as confidential. I want the world to know.

DAVID: When I asked if your husband and Dr Furtwängler were colleagues, you said, 'No, that's just the point.' What did you mean exactly?

TAMARA: (*Distraught*) I can't remember what I wanted to say now. It's gone out of my mind. (*She rummages in her handbag.*) I have a list here, why did I bring this list?

DAVID: Perhaps it would help if I asked you questions –

TAMARA: I think Dr Furtwängler is the only man who can give me proof that my husband existed.

DAVID: How could he do that?

TAMARA: I've not been well. For some years now I've not been well. After they took Walter – we were in Paris at the time – I returned here to be near my mother. My father was with the army of occupation in Denmark. I shall be thirty-three next birthday, look at my hair – (*She holds out a strand of hair.*) I'm trying to return to France but the French authorities are not helpful. I want to die in Paris. It was the only place we were happy.

ARNOLD: (*Gently*) Tamara, where are you staying? Because I'll have you taken back there and then I can get a doctor to you, and –

TAMARA: (*To* DAVID, *ignoring* ARNOLD) I was a philosophy student in 1932, at the University here in Berlin. I was eighteen years old. I was taken to a recital in a private house to hear a young pianist. The house belonged to Dr Myra Samuel, who was a famous piano teacher of the time. The young pianist was Walter Sachs, aged seventeen. A year younger than me. I fell in love with him just listening to him play. He was very beautiful. We were married. He was a Jew. I am not. My maiden name was Müller.

ARNOLD: Just tell us how Dr Furtwängler figures in all this.

TAMARA: It's an outrage what you are doing, you know.

ARNOLD: What are we doing?

TAMARA: Behaving like them.

DAVID: What happened to your husband, Mrs Sachs?

TAMARA: He died. In Auschwitz. That's in Poland. I don't know the exact date.

DAVID: And Dr Furtwängler?

TAMARA: We were tipped off that my husband was to be arrested within the week. We had no money, no influence. We went rushing round to Myra Samuel. We asked for help. She said she'd see what she could do. That evening she sent a message: be at such-and-such an address at midnight. It was a cellar, once a nightclub but closed down. We were terrified. We knocked. Dr Samuel opened the door and admitted us. There was only one other

person there. 'This is Wilhelm Furtwängler,' she said. 'He
will listen to you play.' There was an old upright piano, a
Bechstein, out of tune. Walter sat down and played no
more than three minutes of the 'Waldstein' Sonata. Dr
Furtwängler suddenly stood. He said, 'I will try to help,'
and left quickly. The very next day we received an official
permit to leave. We took the train to Paris and we were
happy. Walter began to make a name for himself. Then.
June, 1940. They took Walter away. I am not Jewish. My
maiden name was Müller – (*She suddenly remembers
something, becomes agitated.*) Yes, yes, I have this list –
(*Rummages in her handbag again, produces sheets of paper.*) I
remember now, these are some of the other people he
helped, Jews and non-Jews he helped. (*Reading.*) Ludwig
Misch, Felix Lederer, Josef Krips, Arnold Schönberg,
dozens and dozens of people he helped. He helped Walter
Sachs, my husband, undoubtedly the finest pianist of his
generation, I'll find out more, I'll keep asking, I'll write
letters, I'll give evidence, because I know what you want to
do, you want to destroy him, isn't that true? You want to
burn him at the stake –

DAVID: We're just trying to find out the truth –

TAMARA: How can you find out the truth? There's no such
thing. Who's truth? The victors? The vanquished? The
victims? The dead? Whose truth? No, no. You have only
one duty. To determine who is good and who is evil. That's
all there is to it. To destroy one good man now is to make
the future impossible. Don't behave like them, please. I
know what I'm talking about, the good are few and far
between. You must honour the good, especially if they are
few. Like Dr Furtwängler. And the children of the good.
Like Fräulein Straube.

ARNOLD: Gee, Emmi, you're really famous in this city.

TAMARA: I want to see him, please. I want to know if he
remembers Walter. I want to know if he remembers that
night Walter played the opening of the 'Waldstein' Sonata
on an out-of-tune Bechstein upright piano in a Berlin cellar.
(DAVID *looks enquiringly at* ARNOLD.)

ARNOLD: Tamara, not today. We have to talk to your
benefactor first, you see?

TAMARA: You're going to set fire to him, aren't you?

ARNOLD: Ah, c'mon, Tamara, I'm only an investigating officer.
I don't have the power to set fire to anybody. Even if I
wanted to. Which I don't. Believe me. Here's what we'll
do. Emmi's going to take you out the back way and she's
going to get Sergeant Bonelli to drive you to wherever you
want to go. (*Writes on a piece of paper.*) This is my number.
I want you to call me if you need anything, I mean
anything, food, cigarettes, medicine, anything, okay?
How's that sound?

TAMARA: It sounds as if you're going to burn him.

ARNOLD: Emmi, take Tamara out the back way.

(EMMI *starts to take* TAMARA *to the door but* TAMARA *stops.*)

TAMARA: Would you like this list? I have a copy.

ARNOLD: You keep it, Tamara, and the copy. But thanks a lot.
(*She goes quickly followed by* EMMI. ARNOLD *gives a yelp of
triumph.*)
Jesus Christ! Are we going to nail him! We're going to nail
him good and proper –
(*He stops, noticing* DAVID's *bewildered expression.*)
You don't see it, do you?

DAVID: No, I don't see how a list of people whom he's supposed
to have helped –

ARNOLD: David, last month I was in Vienna. I had with me an
Austrian driver, Max his name was, he'd done time in the
camps. We were looking at these Viennese cleaning up the
bomb damage, scavenging for rotting food, butt ends,
anything. I said, 'To think, a million of these people came
out to welcome Adolf on the day he entered the city, a
million of them, and now look at 'em.' And Max said, 'Oh
not these people, Major. These people were all at home
hiding Jews in their attics.' You get the point, David? The
point is they're all full of shit.

DAVID: If I may say so, Major, I think Dr Furtwängler's in a
different category. He is, after all, one of the most famous
conductors in the world –

ARNOLD: (*Interrupting*) I'm going to tell you another story, David. Before I got this assignment, I was at Ike's headquarters, interrogating prisoners of war. Then they sent for me. They said, 'You ever heard of Wilhelm Furtwängler?' 'No,' I said. 'You heard of Toscanini?' 'Sure,' I said. 'You heard of Stockowski?' 'Yeah,' I said, 'I heard of him, old guy with white hair, looks like Harpo Marx's grandpa.' 'That's the one,' they said, 'and this guy Furtwängler's bigger than both of them.' 'I get it,' I said, 'the guy's a band leader.' They laughed, oh boy, they really laughed. They said, well, he may be more than that, Steve. In this neck of the woods he's probably Bob Hope and Betty Grable rolled into one. 'Jeez,' I said, 'and I never heard of him.' And you know what they said next? They said, 'Steve, that's why you get the job.'

DAVID: Who's 'they', Major?

ARNOLD: Who's they what?

DAVID: Who's the 'they' that sent for you? Who's the 'they' that gave you this assignment?

ARNOLD: There's no 'the they', David. I'm just doing my job. And always remember we're dealing here with degenerates, that's all you got to remember. I seen things with these eyes –
(*He shudders.* DAVID *watches him.*)

DAVID: Major –

ARNOLD: Steve, c'mon, please –

DAVID: Don't treat me as if I'm not on your side.

ARNOLD: Well, I do that, David, because I don't yet know what side you're on.

DAVID: I think that's insulting –

ARNOLD: Tough. Hank Greenwood gave me the same feeling. He was interested in justice, evidence, facts. I'm interested in nailing the bastard –
(EMMI *returns.*)
Did Bonelli find her transport?

EMMI: Yes.

ARNOLD: Okay. This is it. Emmi, go get him.
(EMMI *exits.*)

Same rules of engagement. I'll explain why he's here, then I'll ask two questions. And then we'll wait. (*Sits at his desk.*) Oh boy, have I been looking forward to this.

(EMMI *re-appears.*)

EMMI: Dr Wilhelm Furtwängler.

(WILHELM FURTWÄNGLER, *wearing a well-cut but worn overcoat, enters. He is sixty, arrogant and remote but at the moment irritated at having been kept waiting. As he passes her,* EMMI *gives him a small curtsey, no more than a bob.* DAVID *inclines his head, a sort of bow.* FURTWÄNGLER *glances round, sees the visitor's chair and sits in it.* ARNOLD *looks up.*)

ARNOLD: Wilhelm, I didn't hear anyone invite you to sit down.

(FURTWÄNGLER *stands;* ARNOLD *points to the other chair.*) Sit there.

(FURTWÄNGLER *sits in the witness chair.*) I'm Steve Arnold. This is David Wills.

(ARNOLD *consults a file.*) Now, Wilhelm, I want you to understand why you're here. You're automatically banned from public life under Control Council Directive No. 24. We're looking into your case before you appear in front of the Tribunal of Artists of the Denazification Commission. You understand that?

FURTWÄNGLER: I have already been cleared by a denazification tribunal in Austria.

ARNOLD: What they do in Austria doesn't interest me one little bit. Okay? I have your questionnaire here. (*Reading.*) Gustav Heinrich Ernst Martin Wilhelm Furtwängler, born Berlin, January, 1886. Orchestral conductor. And you say here you never joined the Party.

FURTWÄNGLER: That is correct.

(*A very long silence;* ARNOLD *waits; nothing from* FURTWÄNGLER; *when the silence is unbearable* ARNOLD *explodes.*)

ARNOLD: Jesus Christ, aren't you going to tell us about carrying your baton in your right hand so you wouldn't have to salute and poke Adolf's eyes out?

(*Nothing from* FURTWÄNGLER.)

And aren't you going to tell us about being a Prussian Privy Councillor? How did that happen to a non-Party member?

FURTWÄNGLER: I received a telegram from Hermann Göring who was Prime Minister of Prussia, this was in 1933, informing me that he had made me a Privy Councillor. I was not given the opportunity either to accept or to refuse. After the dreadful events of November, '38, the violent attacks against Jews, I stopped using the title.

ARNOLD: Great, great, you stopped using the title, and what about Vice-President of the Chamber of Music, you used that title, didn't you, but then I suppose you had no choice there either, because I suppose Josef just sent you a telegram saying, Dear Mr Vice-President.

FURTWÄNGLER: No. I don't think Goebbels sent me a telegram. I was simply told. In a letter, I think. I don't remember exactly –

ARNOLD: You don't remember exactly, okay, but, hell, Hermann and Josef were sure heaping honours on you. One makes you a Privy Councillor, the other makes you Vice-President of the Chamber of Music, and you weren't even a member of the Party, how do you explain that?

FURTWÄNGLER: There was a constant battle between Göring and Goebbels as to which of them would control Nazi culture. People like me, and Richard Strauss, were simply in the middle. We were pawns. Anyway, I resigned from the Chamber of Music at the same time as I resigned as Musical Director of the Berlin Philharmonic Orchestra. In 1934.

DAVID: Why was that? Why did you resign, Dr Furtwängler?

(ARNOLD *shoots* DAVID *a sharp look of annoyance.*)

FURTWÄNGLER: They came to power in January '33. In April, I wrote an open letter to the newspapers condemning what they were doing to music, making these distinctions between Jews and non-Jews. For my part, the only divide in art is between good and bad. Great artists are rare, I said, and no country can do without them unless it wishes to damage its cultural life irrevocably. I also said that men like Otto Klemperer, Bruno Walter, Max Reinhardt, I may

have mentioned others, I don't remember now, must be
allowed to serve their art here in this country.

DAVID: And then you resigned?

FURTWÄNGLER: No, not then. Those were early days. No, the
matter came to a head when Goebbels decided to ban *Mathis
the Painter*, an opera by Paul Hindemith. They called it
Jew-infected Bolshevik music, or some such nonsense. Again
I wrote to the newspapers. Again I criticized them. Goebbels
retaliated with a speech in which he denounced me for what
he called 'my disloyalty to the regime'. That's when I
resigned. I resigned everything. I simply withdrew from
public life and started composing again, which I'd always
thought was my true vocation. Eventually, after much toing
and froing, I was summoned by Goebbels. He said I could
leave the country if I wanted to but under no condition
would I ever be allowed to return. That would have been a
victory for them. I believe you have to fight from inside not
from without. He then demanded I acknowledge Hitler as
solely responsible for cultural policy. Well, that was a fact.
He was the sole arbiter and it seemed to me pointless to deny
it. In return, I demanded I be allowed to stay here, to work,
but I would not be obliged to accept any official position.
Nor would I have to perform at state functions. I have always
held the view that art and politics should have nothing to do
with each other.

ARNOLD: Oh, really? Then why did you conduct at one of their
Nürnberg rallies?

FURTWÄNGLER: (*Flaring*) I did not conduct at the rally, I
conducted on the evening *before* the rally –

ARNOLD: That sounds like the small print in one of our insurance
policies, Wilhelm –

FURTWÄNGLER: I had nothing to do with the rally.

ARNOLD: And what about April 19, 1942? The eve of Adolf's
fifty-third birthday, the big night, the big celebration, you
conducted for Adolf, didn't you? Was that in keeping with
your view that art and politics have nothing to do with each
other?

FURTWÄNGLER: (*Flustered*) That was a different matter –

ARNOLD: I'll believe that —

FURTWÄNGLER: I was tricked —

ARNOLD: How come?

FURTWÄNGLER: I was in Vienna, rehearsing the Ninth
Symphony of Beethoven with the Vienna Philharmonic
when Goebbels called and said I had to conduct at Hitler's
birthday. Always, I'd managed to wriggle out of such
invitations, pleading previous engagements, illness, and so
on. I was also fortunate that Baldur von Schirach, who
controlled Vienna, hated Goebbels and would do anything to
thwart his wishes. He had often helped me in the past by
saying, for example, that he had the prior claim on my
services. But on this particular occasion, in 1942, Goebbels
got to my doctors before me, they were frightened off, and
von Schirach was threatened and bullied and gave in. I had
no alternative but to conduct for Hitler. Believe me, I knew I
had compromised, and I deeply regret it.

ARNOLD: (*Playing with him*) Von Schirach, von Schirach. Is that
the same Baldur von Schirach, the Nazi Youth Leader,
who's now sitting in the dock at Nürnberg, on trial for his
life, charged with crimes against humanity?
(*No response.*)
So that's how you were 'tricked', huh? Doesn't sound much
of a trick to me.

FURTWÄNGLER: To the best of my knowledge that is what
happened. The trick was that pressure was brought to bear
before I was able to manoeuvre. The regime knew as well as I
did that I had not bowed my knee.

ARNOLD: It doesn't sound like that to me. It sounds like you
made a deal —

FURTWÄNGLER: I made no deal. My only concern was preserving
the highest musical standards. That I believe to be my
mission.

ARNOLD: I don't buy that —

FURTWÄNGLER: It's the truth —

ARNOLD: Do you remember a pianist called Walter Sachs?

FURTWÄNGLER: No.

ARNOLD: A young, Jewish pianist?

FURTWÄNGLER: No.

ARNOLD: A pupil of – (*To* EMMI.) What was the teacher's name?

EMMI: Myra Samuel –

FURTWÄNGLER: I knew Myra Samuel –

ARNOLD: And you don't remember this pupil of hers playing to you in a cellar, here in Berlin?

FURTWÄNGLER: Vaguely. What was his name?

ARNOLD: Walter Sachs.

FURTWÄNGLER: Sachs, Sachs –

ARNOLD: His widow attacked you a minute ago –

FURTWÄNGLER: No one's attacked me –

ARNOLD: In the waiting-room –

FURTWÄNGLER: But that woman didn't attack me. She was trying to kiss my hand.

ARNOLD: Right. Right. I guess that was because she's grateful to you. She wanted to thank you for helping her husband. You got him a permit to leave for Paris. How did you do that, Wilhelm?

FURTWÄNGLER: I can't remember. There were so many.

ARNOLD: Yeah, yeah, we've heard about all the folks you helped. I'm just interested in how you went about it. Did you call someone you knew?

FURTWÄNGLER: I may have, as I say, I simply don't remember.

ARNOLD: Let me guess then. You picked up the phone and made a call. (*Mimes a telephone.*) 'Hi, Adolf? Wilhelm speaking. Listen, old pal, there's a Jew-boy pianist I want you to help. He needs a permit to get to Paris. Gee, that's swell of you, Adolf. Shall I have him pick it up or will you send it round? God bless you, Adolf, and Heil fucking Hitler!'
(EMMI *sticks her fingers in her ears and shuts her eyes tight.*)
Or maybe you called Hermann or Josef? Because, you see, I think you made a deal, you shook hands with the Devil and you became real close to him and his cohorts. You were so close you were in the same shithouse as them, you could wipe their asses for them –
(*He suddenly notices* EMMI.)
Emmi, how the hell can you take notes with your goddam fingers – ? Emmi!

(*She removes her fingers.*)

This is Emmi Straube, Wilhelm. She's a very sensitive girl.
(FURTWÄNGLER *gives her a nod.*)

So, Wilhelm, how many Jews do you think you helped?

FURTWÄNGLER: I have no idea.

ARNOLD: That many, huh?

FURTWÄNGLER: I am not going to defend myself by trumpeting numbers. May I ask a question?

ARNOLD: Sure.

FURTWÄNGLER: When will my case be heard by the Tribunal?

ARNOLD: Your guess is as good as mine.

FURTWÄNGLER: I recently visited your colleagues in Wiesbaden, the American Occupation Authorities, those charged with assisting my defense, they were extremely polite and helpful. They said they –

ARNOLD: This isn't Wiesbaden. And I'm not here to defend you –

FURTWÄNGLER: I need to work. I need to make my living. I have been living off the generosity of friends –

ARNOLD: Tough, but these things take time –

FURTWÄNGLER: (*Growing more and more agitated*) Then why is it, please, that – that – another conductor who was actually a member of the Party, I believe he joined twice, why has he already been cleared and is working again, while I have to wait and wait and wait?

ARNOLD: I don't know who he is, he wasn't my case –

FURTWÄNGLER: And why is it, please, that on good authority I have learned that certain high-ranking Nazi scientists are, even as we speak, being transported to the United States to work on missiles and rocket fuels?

ARNOLD: That's what we call the spoils of war, Wilhelm. Different professions, different rules. Why did you escape to Switzerland in January last year?

FURTWÄNGLER: What?

ARNOLD: Why did you escape to Switzerland last year?

FURTWÄNGLER: Because I learned that the Gestapo were about to arrest me.

ARNOLD: Why were they going to arrest you?

FURTWÄNGLER: I'm not absolutely sure but I believe it was

because of another letter I'd written to Goebbels lamenting the decline of musical standards due to racial policies.

ARNOLD: You didn't complain about the racial policies, just about the decline of musical standards, is that right?

(*No response.*)

So, how did you learn that the Gestapo was out to get you?

FURTWÄNGLER: During an enforced hour-long interval, because of a power failure at a concert in the Blüthner Hall, here, in Berlin, Albert Speer, the Minister of Armaments, said to me, casually, 'You look very tired, Maestro, you should go abroad for a while.' I understood exactly what he meant.

ARNOLD: (*Affecting innocence*) Is that the same Albert Speer who's now sitting beside your other friend, Baldur, in the dock at Nürnberg, also charged with crimes against humanity?

(*No response.*)

You sure knew a lot of people in high places.

FURTWÄNGLER: It would be truer to say that a lot of people in high places knew me.

ARNOLD: Don't get smart with me, because your friends seem to be just a bunch of criminal shitheads. But I know and you know that you were real close to all of them, to Adolf and Hermann and Josef and Baldur and now Albert. Make a call, a Jew is saved. Write a nasty letter, Albert says leave town. So, let's hear the truth, Wilhelm, let's come clean. What was your Party number?

FURTWÄNGLER: If you are going to bully me like this, Major, then you had better do your homework. You obviously have no idea how stupid and impertinent your remarks are.

ARNOLD: (*Stung*) You remember, David, I said I had a question for Wilhelm that he wouldn't be able to answer. Well, I'm going to ask it now. You ready for this, Wilhelm? Take your time, it's a tough one. Why didn't you get out right at the start when Adolf came to power in 1933? I have some names here, people in your line of business, who got out in '33. Bruno Walter, Otto Klemperer –

FURTWÄNGLER: But they were Jews, they had to leave, they were right to leave.

(*Brief silence.*)

I love my country and my people. That is a matter of body and soul. I could not leave my country in her deepest misery. To have left in 1933 or '34 would have been shameful. I remained here to give comfort, to see that the glorious musical tradition, of which I believe I am one of the guardians, remained unbroken, was intact when we woke from the nightmare. I remained because I believed my place was with my people.

ARNOLD: See, David? He can't answer the question. I'll ask it again, Wilhelm, and don't give me any more airy-fairy bullshit –

FURTWÄNGLER: (*Flaring, at his most arrogant*) I have told you my reasons, and I only hope, Major, you will be as hard on other artists who have remained in their countries. Shostakovich, Prokofiev, Eisenstein, especially Eisenstein with his films glorifying tyranny, but you could accuse them all of glorifying tyranny –

ARNOLD: I never heard of them, they're not on my list –

DAVID: No, they're Russians –

ARNOLD: Russians? (*Laughs.*) Yeah, Russians –

(*The telephone rings.*)

EMMI: (*Into telephone*) Major Arnold's office. (*Listens.*) It's Major Richards for Lieutenant Wills.

DAVID: (*Taking the telephone*) Wills. (*Listens.*) Yes. You want me to tell him? Yup. (*To* ARNOLD.) Major Richards wants a word.

(ARNOLD *goes to the small table with the telephone extension.* EMMI *waits for him to pick up, then puts down her receiver.* FURTWÄNGLER *rises.*)

FURTWÄNGLER: I have had enough of this. I am leaving now.

DAVID: I don't think that would be advisable.

(FURTWÄNGLER *hesitates and doesn't leave.* ARNOLD *yelps with delight and then laughs.* DAVID *summons his courage.*)

DAVID: Dr Furtwängler.

(FURTWÄNGLER *turns to him;* DAVID *feels awkward but takes the plunge as though he's been preparing a speech.*)

When I was ten, in 1932, my father, he was a publisher, allowed me to accompany him on a business trip to Berlin.

On the second evening of our visit, he took me to the Philharmonic. I can't remember the whole programme but I do remember you conducted both Beethoven's *Egmont* overture and the Fifth Symphony. I think the concert ended with the overture to Tannhaüser. You opened a new world to me –

(*Another yelp and laughter from* ARNOLD; DAVID *falters, searching now for the words.*)

More than a world. Like waking from sleep. A child of ten. Waking to a new world. You showed me a place where there was – an absence of misery. Ever since I first heard you, music has been central to my life. My chief comfort. And I've needed comfort. I thank you for that.

(*He stops, embarrassed, turns away.* FURTWÄNGLER *nods, smiles sadly. Again* ARNOLD *laughs.*)

EMMI: I, too. The same. Thank you.

(FURTWÄNGLER *gives her a wonderful smile. She looks away.*)

FURTWÄNGLER: Fräulein – ?

EMMI: Straube.

FURTWÄNGLER: Wann haben *Sie* mich zum ersten mal als Dirigent erlebt?

EMMI: (*Mumbling*) Hier. In Berlin. Neunzehnhundertdreiundvierzig –

FURTWÄNGLER: (*Not having heard; gently*) Wann?

(ARNOLD *puts down the telephone, dangerously pleased with himself.*)

ARNOLD: I've got to hand it to the British, David. You know what those guys are? Decent. Wilhelm, tell me, do you know Hans Hinkel?

FURTWÄNGLER: Do I know Hans Hinkel?

ARNOLD: Why does everybody repeat my questions?

FURTWÄNGLER: Do I know Hans Hinkel?

ARNOLD: See? There he goes again –

FURTWÄNGLER: Yes, I know him. A despicable human being. Ask Bruno Walter. It was Hinkel who personally drove him out. You know what his job was in the Ministry of Culture? To get rid of Jews in the arts, and since the most talented artists were inevitably Jewish, he was seldom idle. I could detail his persecution of my former secretary, Berta Geissmar, herself a Jewess, but I will not bore you with a chronicle of cruelty, meanness and mendacity.

ARNOLD: Yup, sounds like the same guy. You know what else this little creep did? He kept files, close on 250,000 files. And you know what's in those files?

FURTWÄNGLER: How should I know –

ARNOLD: Oh boy, you're going to love this. Those files contain – wait for this – the details of every artist working in this country for – guess who? That's right, Wilhelm, your old pals, Adolf and Josef and Hermann. These files are going to tell us when all of you joined the Party, who informed and who was helpful and, what's more, they're full of love letters to your aforementioned pals, swearing everlasting loyalty. Isn't that something? A file on every one of you. Some guy, that Hinkel.

FURTWÄNGLER: I should like to leave now.

ARNOLD: I bet you would, so why don't you? See, we have work to do sifting through those files, and that'll take some time, I guess. So, get out of here. And we'll call you back when we're good and ready.

(FURTWÄNGLER *goes to the door but stops, turns to* EMMI *and gives a bow and a smile, then goes.* ARNOLD *hurries to his desk.*) We've got him! See how the moment I mentioned Hinkel he wanted out? Boy, oh boy! Emmi, give David a list of the witnesses, and get us some more coffee, will you? David, here's what I want you to do. (*He finds files and hands them to* DAVID.) These are pretty well verbatims of my interrogations. We'll compare the answers the shitheads gave me with the info in Hinkel's files. This is an Aladdin's cave. Jesus, when you think the Russians had the whole archive in their hands until the city was divided and they didn't know what it was. You know what they'll be doing now? Shitting razor blades.

(*During this,* EMMI, *on her way to the door, has put on a record and then turns up the volume: the opening of Beethoven's Eighth Symphony at full blast. She goes quickly.*)

ARNOLD: Hey, turn that off, we can't hear ourselves think. (*Looks up, realizes she's gone.*) David, turn that off.
(DAVID *pretends not to hear.*)
Shit.
(ARNOLD *rises, crosses to the record player and as he takes off the record the music stops abruptly.*
Blackout.)

ACT TWO

SCENE ONE

April. 10 p.m. Warm spring evening. Dim light from the desk lamp.
RODE *stands in the double doorway, having just greeted* ARNOLD. *He
wears a tattered cardigan over a short-sleeved shirt and slacks.*
ARNOLD *is at his desk which is covered in paper. He is inwardly
excited, his mood dangerous.* RODE *carries a slender leather case.*

RODE: (*Beaming*) Major, you must now guess what I am holding
   in my hand.

ARNOLD: Your dick.

RODE: No, no, come now, guess. You like guessing games?

ARNOLD: Love 'em. I give up, what you holding in your hand,
   Helmuth?

RODE: (*Glancing round nervously*) No Fräulein Straube?

ARNOLD: No. That's because I wanted to see you alone,
   Helmuth. Off the record. So what you got there?

RODE: You can't guess?
   (*He opens the leather case.*)

ARNOLD: Helmuth, I think I know what it is.

RODE: What?

ARNOLD: A telescope. For spying on people. Right?

RODE: (*A little uneasy, a nervous smile*) No, no, no, not at all. (*He
   takes from the case a conductor's baton.*)

ARNOLD: (*Toying with him*) By Jimminy! A white stick. For the
   blind!

RODE: No, Major, not a white stick, a baton. A conductor's
   baton. And not just *a* baton. *The* baton. My guilty secret.
   The Maestro's baton which I stole.

ARNOLD: The one he kept in his right hand.

RODE: You remember!

ARNOLD: How could I forget? (*Taking the baton.*) Will you look at
   this? I'm holding the baton he kept in his right hand so he
   didn't have to salute and poke Adolf's eyes out.
   (*Suddenly thrusting it at* RODE.)
   Show me, Helmuth.

RODE: Show you?

31

ARNOLD: Yeah, show me. I want to see you do it. C'mon, Helmuth, take the baton.

(RODE *reluctantly takes the baton.* ARNOLD *gets out a comb, flicks a lock of hair over his forehead and holds the comb under his nose to make a Hitler moustache.*)

Pretend I'm Adolf. You're the Maestro. C'mon. You've got the baton in your right hand but you give me the salute just the same.

RODE: No, really, Major, I don't like giving the salute even in –

ARNOLD: (*Sweetly*) Do it, Helmuth.

(RODE *gives a half-hearted salute.*)

Do it right, Helmuth.

(RODE *gives the salute.*)

You look great doing that, Helmuth, and I see what you mean. You almost poked my eyes out.

RODE: Exactly. (*Puts the baton back in the case and gives it to* ARNOLD.) Perhaps you will do me a favour, Major. If you are seeing the Maestro again, be so good as to return the baton to him. It is, after all, his property. But please don't tell him who took it.

ARNOLD: Don't worry, Helmuth, it'll be our secret.

RODE: In the meantime, you can practise conducting. I saw you had some of our records. (*He glances at the records.*) I am on this one, the Ninth, second fiddle, difficult to identify me exactly. (*He chuckles.*) You're working late tonight. You don't usually see people this late –

ARNOLD: All in the cause of humanity, Helmuth. Or should I call you one–zero–four–nine–three–three–one.

RODE: (*Shaken*) What?

ARNOLD: One–zero–four–nine–three–three–one. Or d'you mind if I just call you 'one'?

(*An agonizing silence: then* RODE *breaks down and sobs.*)

You know what I say you are, Helmuth? I say you're a piece of shit.

RODE: (*Through his sobs*) The bastard, the bastard –

ARNOLD: Who's the bastard, Helmuth? Hinkel?

(RODE *nods.*)

Why? Well, why particularly?

RODE: He said – he said there'd be no records – no file –

ARNOLD: He promised to remove your file?

(*No response.*)

And you thought we'd never find out.

(*No response.*)

You thought we'd never find out that you were the Party's man in the orchestra? Hinkel's man.

(RODE *sobs.*)

Oh, don't take on so, Helmuth. You've only got one Party number. A guy called Herbert von Karajan's got two. (*He laughs.*) By the way, why d'you think he joined the Party twice? Once in Austria, once here? Guess he just wanted them to know he cared, huh?

(*No response.*)

So, c'mon, Party member, one–zero–four–nine–three–three–one, talk to me.

RODE: (*Trying to regain his dignity*) I – I – have confessed my sins. I have been given absolution.

ARNOLD: Yeah, but don't you guys have to do penance? What's your penance, Helmuth?

RODE: Living out the rest of my life.

ARNOLD: Hold it, your story moves me deeply, let me wipe away my tears. I'm so choked up, I can't speak.

RODE: (*Burst of anger*) You don't know what it's like to wake up to a power so terrifying, so immense, that all you can think of is you have to be part of it otherwise you will be eaten alive. And here's something else you won't understand. Absolute power offers absolute certainty and absolute hope.

ARNOLD: Doesn't matter if I understand or not, just get it off your chest, Helmuth.

RODE: And you will never have even the slightest inkling of how corrupt the power was, yes, corrupt and corrupting. You have never experienced a Reign of Terror, so there is no way I can make it clear to you. You start by censoring what you say, then you censor what you think, and you end by censoring what you feel. That is the greatest degradation because it means the entire individual will is paralyzed, and all that remains is an obedient husk. In my case – (*He breaks off.*)

33

ARNOLD: Yeah, go on, Helmuth, in your case?

RODE: It began with a realization.

ARNOLD: And what was that, Helmuth?

RODE: That I am not the best violinist in the world.

ARNOLD: You're not?

RODE: I would never, in my wildest dreams, have been even a second violinist in the Berlin Philharmonic. When they got rid of the – the Jews in the orchestra there were vacancies for people like me. I believed that to be just. I can trace my ancestry back to the thirteenth century.

ARNOLD: I'm told a lot of Jews can go back even further than that.

RODE: (*Suddenly agitated*) I lied about something.

ARNOLD: You surprise me, Helmuth.

RODE: No, no, I have to set the record straight. I told you it was my idea the Maestro should carry the baton in his right hand. Well, it wasn't my idea at all. The idea came from Franz Jastrau. He was the orchestra's handyman.

ARNOLD: Gee, that sure changes the whole picture, Helmuth.

RODE: I don't think the Maestro even knows of my existence. Second violin. A conductor is also a dictator, you know, he is also a terrifying power who gives hope and certainty, and guarantees order. I wanted to be in the Maestro's power, too. The orchestra is a symbol, you see –

ARNOLD: No more philosophy, please, Helmuth, because I want to talk to you about something practical. You ever heard of plea bargaining?

(RODE *shakes his head*.)

Talk about power, I have the power to let you go find work, at least in the American Zone. I could give you a job tomorrow, here, in this building. But I'd have to get something in return. See, Helmuth? That's plea bargaining.

(*Silence.*)

I have to admit, I thought I'd find a great big fat file on the Maestro. I thought, never mind two Party numbers, he'd have three. But his file is just full of letters asking Josef to help this Jew or that Jew.

RODE: Yes, they used to say, there was not a Jew left in Germany whom Furtwängler had not helped.

ARNOLD: C'mon, Helmuth, I can hand you a letter giving you freedom of movement, freedom to work, freedom, Helmuth. Better than scavenging for food in the ruins. But I need something in return. How's that for penance?

RODE: He is an anti-Semite. Of course.

ARNOLD: (*Gently; wheedling*) Of course. But I need facts, Helmuth, hard facts. You have to tell me where to look.

RODE: Major, we're discussing a man of genius here, I don't want – he's one of the greatest conductors alive, maybe *the* greatest –

ARNOLD: Fuck that, Helmuth. You want to discuss symbols here? This guy was a front man. He was the piper but he played their tune, you get my philosophical meaning? I'm not interested in small fish, I'm after Moby Dick. Come on, Helmuth. At least tell me what to look for and where to look for it. Hard facts.

RODE: You ever heard of Vittorio de Sabata?

ARNOLD: No.

RODE: Italian.

ARNOLD: You're kidding.

RODE: A conductor. Front rank. Furtwängler said something like, 'It's impudent for that Jew Sabata to conduct Brahms.'

ARNOLD: Doesn't knock me out that, Helmuth.

RODE: There's a letter –

ARNOLD: Now I'm hearing music, I like letters –

RODE: It must be in the files somewhere – to Cultural Minister Bernhard Rust, I think – full of – full of the sort of thing you're looking for – about Arnold Schönberg – a Jew – you know who I mean?

(ARNOLD *shakes his head*.)

A composer – modern – atonal.

ARNOLD: What's the date of the letter?

RODE: I'll have to think, early I guess, before the war, but – but there's something else I just remembered –

ARNOLD: Yeah?

RODE: Furtwängler sent Hitler a birthday telegram –

ARNOLD: He did?

RODE: Yes. Oddly enough, I had this from one of your people –

35

ARNOLD: From one of my people?

RODE: Yes. A Corporal. US Army. A Jew. He said he'd seen the telegram. In the Chancellery.

ARNOLD: Son-of-a-gun. We'll find the corporal and we'll find the telegram –

RODE: I don't remember his name, but I'll think, it'll come back to me –

ARNOLD: I want you to write all this down, Helmuth.

(*Puts a pad and pen before him.*)

And I want you to think about this. I just know a deal was made, early on. They said, 'Wilhelm, you don't have to join the Party, but just do as we tell you and you won't have to worry about a goddam thing.' And that's why he never left. But I need documentary proof. You know of anything like that?

RODE: No. And if I may say so, Major, I think you're barking up the wrong tree.

ARNOLD: Oh? And what's the right tree, Helmuth?

RODE: There's a pattern to his behaviour, you see. Goebbels understood. And Hinkel. I can tell you things – there's a rumour – I don't know if it's true or not – but ask him about von der Null.

ARNOLD: Never heard of him, who is he?

RODE: Edwin von der Null. A music critic. He was the one who gave Furtwängler terrible reviews while he raved about Herbert von Karajan, the two-time member of the Party. Called him 'The Miracle Karajan'. Furtwängler was outraged and they say he had von der Null conscripted into the army. The same thing happened to another critic, Walter Steinhauer. He savaged Furtwängler in print for not playing more contemporary music. After that review appeared, he too was conscripted. True or not, it's not such a bad idea. Critics give you bad reviews, you have them sent to the Russian front. (*Chuckles.*) But if you really want to get Furtwängler, ask him about Herbert von Karajan.

ARNOLD: This Miracle Kid?

RODE: Yes, that, I believe, will prove fruitful. (*He starts to write.*) Yes, ask him about von Karajan. And you may notice, that

36

he cannot even bring himself to utter the name.
Furtwängler refers to him as K. And ask him about his
private life.

ARNOLD: His private life?
(*Blackout.*)

SCENE TWO

Mid-July. 8.45 a.m. High summer. Intense heat. ARNOLD *is at his
desk. He is half-asleep, head lolling. He suddenly wakes and cries
out. He becomes aware of his surroundings, stares into space with a
distant, forlorn expression.* EMMI *enters carrying a record album.
She is glowing.*

EMMI: I've got it, Major.

ARNOLD: Swell.

EMMI: The British were most helpful. They really have a
broadcasting station there. And they found it for me. Took
no more than ten minutes. Amazing. And I am so pleased
you are becoming interested in serious music, Major.

ARNOLD: Don't let one record fool you, Emmi.

EMMI: But Bruckner's Seventh Symphony, that's difficult even
for me. Should we play it now?

ARNOLD: No, Emmi, not now. You know what they mean by
the Slow Movement?

EMMI: Of course.

ARNOLD: That's the one I want to hear. Put it on ready to play,
and I'll tell you when to play it –

EMMI: I never thought you would ask to listen to Bruckner –

ARNOLD: Well, maybe I'm mellowing. Or maybe the heat's
getting to me. And, wouldn't you know it? We shiver
through a God-awful winter and now the sun's shining the
central heating's working. The military, God bless 'em. No
sign of the band leader?

EMMI: I wish you'd call him Dr Furtwängler. No, he isn't here
but then it's not yet nine o'clock.
(*She peers at him.*)
Are you nervous, Major?

37

ARNOLD: I wish you'd call me Steve, Emmi. No, I'm not nervous, I'm just not getting enough sleep. Bad dreams. And that's when I'm awake.

(*He smiles; she sits at her desk.*)

Now, Emmi, if you want to be out of the room while I talk to him that's okay by me. What I have to say to him may upset you. And, I guess, working for me, you get upset enough.

EMMI: What are you going to say to him, Major?

ARNOLD: Emmi, go for a walk. It's a lovely day out there. Walk in the Tiergarten, sit under what's left of the linden trees, David can take notes.

EMMI: Major, you upset me when you avoid answering my questions –

(*A knock at the door.*)

ARNOLD: See who it is, Emmi, and if it's the band leader don't let him in yet.

(EMMI *opens the door to* RODE *who is dressed in a janitor's overall and cap that somehow looks like a uniform. He carries a small but bulging canvas sack. He bows.*)

Attention! Security! Watch out, Emmi, he may want to frisk you.

RODE: Major, a woman left this for you.

ARNOLD: What woman?

RODE: I don't know her name. She talked to Sergeant Adams on the door and he gave me this and said it was for you.

ARNOLD: Did you see her?

RODE: Of course. I was standing here, Sergeant Adams was there, the woman was no more than –

ARNOLD: (*Interrupting*) What she look like?

(RODE *shrugs*.)

Old, young, fat, thin, short, tall?

RODE: No. (RODE *chuckles*.)

ARNOLD: Okay, very funny, so what's in the package?

RODE: I don't know, Major. Sergeant Adams said it was for you –

ARNOLD: Jesus Christ, Helmuth, you're supposed to be the security in this building –

RODE: But I was not told to open packages addressed to military
    personnel –
ARNOLD: Security, Helmuth, use your goddam common sense –
RODE: Sergeant Adams said I must search people, he did not say I
    must search packages –
ARNOLD: Jesus Christ, no wonder you were a second violinist. I
    mean, it stands to reason. A woman leaves a package for me,
    you got to be curious as to what's in it –
RODE: Why should I be curious? It's addressed to you, Major –
ARNOLD: Because it could be a fucking bomb, Helmuth –
RODE: A bomb? You think so?
ARNOLD: Yes, I think so. Open it.
    (RODE *hesitates*.)
    That's an order, Helmuth. Open it.
    (RODE *hesitates*. EMMI *is apprehensive and ducks a little behind
    her typewriter*. ARNOLD *does not move*.)
RODE: If it's a bomb, Major, shouldn't you take cover?
ARNOLD: Open it.
    (*Gingerly,* RODE *opens the sack*.)
    Well, feel around inside. Go on, Helmuth, feel around.
    (RODE *feels inside the sack*.)
RODE: It just feels like paper, Major.
ARNOLD: Empty it.
    (RODE *is about to do so on Arnold's desk*.)
    On the floor, Helmuth.
    (RODE *empties the sack. Fifty or so envelopes, various sizes and
    colours, cascade on to the floor*.)
    What the hell's that?
    (*All three look at the envelopes, puzzled*.)
RODE: Could be fan mail, Major. I remember with the Maestro –
ARNOLD: Helmuth, who's going to send *me* fan mail for
    Chrissake? Jesus! Emmi, take a look. Helmuth, get back on
    duty. The Russians may launch an attack any moment.
    (RODE *bows smartly and goes*. EMMI *goes down on her knees and
    starts to examine the envelopes*.)
ARNOLD: Well, Emmi?
EMMI: They're all addressed to Mrs Tamara Sachs. And they're
    all open –

ARNOLD: What? I don't get it –

(EMMI *starts to look at the envelopes, then stops.*)

EMMI: Major, can I ask you something?

ARNOLD: The answer's yes, Emmi, I love you, I want you to marry me, and I want you to be the mother of my children, not necessarily in that order.

EMMI: Major!

ARNOLD: What's in those letters, Emmi?

EMMI: No, I want to ask you this. Why have you been so kind to Mr Rode and not so kind to Dr Furtwängler?

ARNOLD: Let's just say I'm a democrat. With a small 'd'. I have more sympathy for the little people. What's in those letters, Emmi?

(DAVID *enters carrying files.*)

DAVID: Good morning –

ARNOLD: Okay, we surrender, the boy scout's here.

DAVID: What's going on?

ARNOLD: Seems like Tamara Sachs's sent me her mail.

DAVID: Why should she do that?

ARNOLD: I don't know exactly. Emmi's trying to come up with an answer.

(DAVID *hands* ARNOLD *the files.*)

DAVID: These are the last of them, Major.

ARNOLD: Anything good?

DAVID: Nothing we didn't know before, but the boys at Wiesbaden have asked me to put some questions to you. And I've found something you're not going to like. I happen to be going through a transcript from the Nürnberg trial –

EMMI: Major?

(ARNOLD *and* DAVID *turn to her.*)

There's one here, unopened. It's addressed, 'To Whom It May Concern'.

ARNOLD: Okay, well, it may concern us, Emmi. Open it. Read it.

(*To* DAVID, *while* EMMI *opens the letter.*)

I said the woman was crazy, didn't I say it? Look at that. Only a crazy woman would send her own mail to whom it may concern.

EMMI: (*Reading*) 'To the American authorities in Wiesbaden and

Berlin. The good and the not so good. I have been busy.
Here are more than fifty letters confirming what I have
already said. Letters, evidence in black and white, from
survivors, widows, lovers, friends, people now mostly in
America and England, all testifying that Wilhelm
Furtwängler was their saviour. Because no one knows when
Dr Furtwängler's case will come before the tribunal and
because I have unexpectedly received permission from the
French authorities to reside in Paris –
(DAVID *shoots* ARNOLD *a look;* ARNOLD *looks blithely
innocent.*)
– I probably will not be here to give evidence on his behalf,
so I have taken copies of these letters. If you destroy them
they will still exist.'
(*Brief silence.* EMMI *continues to sort through the letters.*)
ARNOLD: Son-of-a-gun. Thanks, Tamara, it's a shame they're all
totally irrelevant.
EMMI: There's one here from Dr Furtwängler. (*Reads, translating
from the German.*) 'Dear Mrs Sachs, Thank you for your
letter. Yes, I remember your husband well. As a matter of
fact, I was reminded of him only the other day. I
remembered the Bechstein was out of tune. He was indeed a
fine pianist. I was deeply distressed to hear of his tragic fate.'
(*Brief silence.*)
ARNOLD: Get them up off the floor, Emmi. (*To* DAVID.) You were
saying the good guys at Wiesbaden had questions for me?
DAVID: (*Consulting notes; summoning courage*) They – they don't
think there's a case against Dr Furtwängler and they want to
know why you're pursuing it.
ARNOLD: Tell them they'll know after they've heard the evidence.
(*Hands* DAVID *a fat file.*)
Take a look through that, you'll see what I mean. Next
question.
DAVID: (*Still tentative*) They think you're being ordered to pursue
Dr Furtwängler, and they want to know who's giving the
orders and why?
ARNOLD: Oh, I get it, you've been talking to them, haven't you,
David? You told them about the 'they' who saw me at Ike's

headquarters. I remember you were so interested in who the 'they' were –

DAVID: Yes, I was asked, I –

ARNOLD: Well, you tell the good guys in Wiesbaden to mind their own goddam business.

DAVID: Are you being ordered, Major?

ARNOLD: What's this about a transcript from Nürnberg?

DAVID: Why, Major? Why Dr Furtwängler? Why him?

ARNOLD: Tell me about Nürnberg.

(*Brief pause.* DAVID *consults one of his own files.*)

DAVID: Yes. A man called Dahlerus, Birger Dahlerus –

ARNOLD: Burger, his name's Burger? What is he, some kind of short-order cook?

DAVID: A Swede, a businessman, he was called to give evidence in Göring's defence –

(*The door suddenly bursts open and* FURTWÄNGLER *enters.*)

FURTWÄNGLER: It is now nine o'clock precisely. I have prepared a statement. I do not intend to be kept waiting again.

(*Uneasy, tense silence.*)

ARNOLD: (*Dangerously calm*) Wilhelm, don't talk to me as if I was a second violinist. Go back into the waiting room, sit down, and *wait*. Miss Straube will come and get you when I am ready to see you. If you're not there when she comes to get you, I'll have you pulled in by the Military Police. Okay, Wilhelm?

(FURTWÄNGLER *hesitates, loses confidence, turns and marches off.* RODE *shrugs apologetically and also goes.*)

(*Incensed, almost losing control*) Jesus God, that prick, that arrogant prick, who the fuck does he think he is? Who the fuck? Who the fuck?

(*He paces.* EMMI *watches him, alarmed.*)

DAVID: Major.

(ARNOLD *doesn't seem to hear.*)

Major.

(ARNOLD *stops pacing;* DAVID *again summons courage.*)

I have a favour to ask you.

ARNOLD: (*Suddenly calm*) Okay, I owe you one.

DAVID: When you question him, could I ask you to treat him with more respect?

ARNOLD: With more what? More what?

DAVID: Respect –

ARNOLD: That's what I thought you said. Respect? Are you kidding?

DAVID: He may just be the greatest conductor of this century and that merits respect.

ARNOLD: Yeah, yeah, great conductor, great artist, that's what everybody keeps telling me, and you know what I say to that?

DAVID: I can guess what you say to that, Major –

ARNOLD: You know what I say he is?

DAVID: Yes, I think I can guess that, too –

ARNOLD: David, I just don't understand a thing about you. You're a Jew. Are you a Jew?

DAVID: Yes, I'm a Jew, I'm also a human being –

ARNOLD: A human being, oh, good, I'm relieved, I thought you were going to say you were a music lover. This man, this great artist has made anti-Semitic remarks like you wouldn't believe, I got letters –

DAVID: (*Interrupting*) Major, Major.
(ARNOLD *is still.*)
Show me a non-Jew who hasn't made anti-Semitic remarks and I'll show you the gates of paradise.

ARNOLD: What is it with you? Where are your feelings, David? Where's your hatred, your disgust? Where's your fucking outrage, David? Think of your parents and then think of him conducting 'Happy Birthday, dear Adolf'. I mean, for Chrissake, whose side are you on?
(*Brief pause.*)
So what's this about the Swede in Nürnberg?

DAVID: It doesn't matter now. It's probably irrelevant.
(*Brief pause.*)

ARNOLD: Okay, Emmi. Go get him. Oh, and Emmi. Don't announce him. Just let him come in.
(*She goes. Uneasy silence while they wait.* EMMI *opens the door for* FURTWÄNGLER *who re-enters.*)

43

Wilhelm! Nice to see you. How are you? Been keeping
well? Not too hot for you? Come in, come in, sit down.
(FURTWÄNGLER, *deeply suspicious, goes for the witness
chair.*)
No, no, take this one, it's more comfortable –
(ARNOLD *places the visitor's chair and holds it for*
FURTWÄNGLER *who sits.*)
Isn't this heat something else? You want to loosen your
tie, take off your jacket? Just relax, because the good news
is that this is the last time you'll have to see me.
(FURTWÄNGLER *eyes him suspiciously.*)
But the bad news is that I still have to test the case against
you, see if it'll stand up, and if it does, then I hand over
to the civil authorities, to your own people, a guy called
Alex Vogel, you ever heard of him?

FURTWÄNGLER: Yes, I've heard of him.

ARNOLD: And what have you heard?

FURTWÄNGLER: That he's a Moscow hack, a communist.

ARNOLD: That's the one. Not a nice man. We are not on first
name terms. So, today, thank your lucky stars, you've
only got me to deal with. Now, let's take it nice and easy.
Okay? I don't want to go over all the old stuff because I
have one or two new things that have come up –

FURTWÄNGLER: (*Interrupting*) I wish to say something.

ARNOLD: Go ahead, be my guest.

FURTWÄNGLER: (*Takes out a piece of paper*) When I last saw
you, I was unprepared, I did not know what to expect. In
the past weeks, I have been thinking more carefully and
making some notes.
(*Glances at notes; more to* DAVID.)
You have to understand who I am and what I am. I am a
musician and I believe in music. I am an artist and I believe
in art. You could say that art is my religion. Art in general,
and music, of course, in particular, has for me mystical
powers which nurture man's spiritual needs. I must
confess, however, to having been extremely naïve. I insisted
for many years, until quite recently in fact, on the absolute
separation of art and politics. I truly had no interest in

politics, I hardly read newspapers, my entire life was devoted to music because, and this is very important, I believed that I could, through music, preserve something practical.

ARNOLD: And what was that?

FURTWÄNGLER: Liberty, humanity and justice.

ARNOLD: Gee, Wilhelm, that's a thing of beauty, honest to God, a thing of beauty. I'm going to try to remember that. How's it go? Liberty, humanity and justice. Beautiful. But you used the word 'naïve'. Are you now saying you think you were wrong? That art and politics can't be separated?

FURTWÄNGLER: I believe they should be kept separate, but that they weren't kept separate I learned to my cost.

ARNOLD: And when did you first learn that? When you sent the telegram? Was that the surrender signal, the waving of the white flag?

FURTWÄNGLER: What telegram?

ARNOLD: 'Happy Birthday, dear Adolf, love Wilhelm.' Or words to that effect. That sounds to me like you were dropping on your knees and saying, 'Okay, Adolf, you win. You're top dog in everything, so let's be pals. Have a swell party.' Is that when you decided you couldn't keep art and politics separate, when you sent the telegram?

FURTWÄNGLER: I have no idea what you're talking about.

ARNOLD: I'm talking about the birthday greetings to your old pal, Adolf.

FURTWÄNGLER: I never sent him birthday greetings or any other kind of greetings.

ARNOLD: Think carefully, Wilhelm –

FURTWÄNGLER: I don't have to think carefully. This is utterly ridiculous. I never sent him a telegram.

(DAVID, *who has been consulting the file* ARNOLD *gave him, raises a discreet finger.*)

ARNOLD: Yes, David?

DAVID: (*Apparently innocently*) Why not show Dr Furtwängler the evidence? It may refresh his memory.

(ARNOLD *shoots* DAVID *a sharp, furious look.*)

I can't seem to find it here, Emmi, perhaps you have the telegram in your files –

EMMI: No, I have never seen such a telegram –

DAVID: Major, if you tell me where the telegram is –

FURTWÄNGLER: You won't find it because no such telegram exists.

(*Ominous silence. Then,* ARNOLD *forces a boisterous laugh.*)

ARNOLD: Well, I tried, you got to admit, I tried. I thought I might just trap you there, Wilhelm, but David here was a little too quick for me. Smart move, David. Smart move. No, I don't have the telegram, but I know it exists. And I just want to tell you. Wilhelm, we're going to keep looking for it because I happen to believe you sent it.

FURTWÄNGLER: Then you are wrong.

(ARNOLD *is not pleased.*)

ARNOLD: Art and politics, yeah, art and politics. Are you saying that touring abroad, conducting the Berlin Philharmonic Orchestra in foreign lands from 1933 on wasn't a commercial for Adolf and all he stood for?

FURTWÄNGLER: We never, never officially represented the regime when we played abroad. We always played as a private ensemble. As I think I already told you, I was a freelance conductor –

ARNOLD: You know something? You should've written our policies for us because you got more exclusion clauses than Double Indemnity. Don't give me fine print again, I'm an expert when it comes to fine print. What d'you imagine people thought? The Berlin Philharmonic's taken over by Josef's Propaganda Ministry but Wilhelm's a freelance, so music and politics are now entirely separate? Is that what you believed ordinary people thought?

FURTWÄNGLER: I have no idea what ordinary people thought –

ARNOLD: No –

FURTWÄNGLER: – because I had only one intention, from 1933 onwards. Whatever I did, and this is also the real reason I did not leave my country, I had only one intention and that was to prove that art means more than politics.

ARNOLD: Did that include Herbert von Karajan?

FURTWÄNGLER: (*Flustered*) What – what – I don't know what you mean –

ARNOLD: Tell me about von der Null.

FURTWÄNGLER: (*Taken off guard*) Von der Null?

ARNOLD: Yes, von der Null –

FURTWÄNGLER: Von der Null –

ARNOLD: How long's this going to go on, Wilhelm? I say von der Null, you say von der Null, I say von der Null, you say von der Null, we could go on all day. You know who von der Null is, don't you? Edwin von der Null, music critic –

FURTWÄNGLER: Yes, I know who he is –

ARNOLD: Isn't it true that because he gave you bad reviews and praised this young guy, von Karajan, called him a goddam miracle, said he was better than you, you had von der Null conscripted into the army and nobody's heard from him since?

FURTWÄNGLER: That's an outrageous lie!

ARNOLD: You sure you didn't call one of your close buddies and say, God in heaven, did you see what that guy von der Null wrote about me? I want him out the way. And the same with that other critic, Steinhauer. He had the nerve to accuse me, the greatest conductor on earth, of not playing enough modern music. Send him to Stalingrad. Isn't that what you did? You don't like criticism, do you? You certainly didn't like them saying there was another conductor who was better than you –

(FURTWÄNGLER *rises angrily*.)

FURTWÄNGLER: (*Exploding; pacing*) Please stop playing these games with me. You seem to take pleasure in teasing and baiting and hectoring me. Have some regard for my intelligence. We are dealing here with matters concerning my entire existence, my career, my life. Why you should introduce the name of – of another conductor is beyond my understanding.

ARNOLD: I'll tell you why. You remember we talked about you playing for Adolf's birthday? And you told me that Josef got to your doctors first, that you were tricked, outflanked?

FURTWÄNGLER: Yes, and that's what happened –

ARNOLD: I have a different story to tell. I don't believe you were tricked. Not in the way you describe. I believe something

47

else happened. I've looked at the Hinkel Archive, made a
few enquiries, I've seen records of phone calls, and putting
it all together, this is what I think happened. I think Josef
said, 'Wilhelm, if you won't conduct for Adolf's birthday,
we'll get the Miracle Kid, the guy that critic von der Nüll
thinks is the greatest conductor in the world, the guy you
call K. He's not just willing to conduct for Adolf, he's
offered to sing "Happy Birthday" as a solo.'
(*Silence.*)
Come on now, Wilhelm, admit it. K worried you, didn't
he? He always worried you. In 1942, he's thirty-four years
old, you're already fifty-six. He's the Young Pretender, the
comet, yeah, the miracle. He's tilting at your throne. Your
position's in danger. And Josef and Hermann keep saying
to you, 'If you don't do it, little K will.' Never mind art
and politics and symbols and airy-fairy bullshit about
liberty, humanity and justice. You were tricked all right,
because they got you where you were most vulnerable.
Youth was knocking on the door, and I don't care how
great you are, how noble, how fantastic with your little
white stick, because it's the oldest story in the book. The
ageing Romeo jealous of the young buck, the Heavyweight
Champion of the World frightened of the Young
Contender. And the great maestro terrified of the new boy
on the podium. Wasn't that how they got you, Wilhelm,
time after time? Admit it. The real reason you didn't leave
the country when you knew you should have was that you
were frightened. You were frightened that, once you were
out of the way, you'd be supplanted by the Miracle Kid,
the Party's boy twice over, flashy, talented little K.
FURTWÄNGLER: This is absolute nonsense –
DAVID: Major, wait a moment, where is this leading? This isn't
    establishing –
ARNOLD: (*Turning on him, cutting him off*) Not now, David, I
    haven't finished with him. As a matter of fact, I've hardly
    begun. I'm only just developing my theme. Isn't that what
    you call it in classical music, developing a theme? Okay,
    Wilhelm, so they played on your insecurity. That's

human, understandable, nothing to be ashamed of. After all, it's pretty well agreed that little K's got what it takes, and nearly everyone in the Party loved him. Jesus, he's a member twice over, he's one of theirs. But, take note of what I said. I said nearly everyone in the Party because there's one exception. One guy doesn't like little K as much as he likes you, there's one guy who thinks little K is not fit to brush your coat tails, and that guy just happens to be – yeah, the number one man, your old pal, Adolf. He thinks you're the greatest and when he says, I want Wilhelm for my birthday party, boy, they better go get Wilhelm. So, Josef calls and threatens you with little K. And you said to hell with the Ninth in Vienna, I'll give it to Adolf as a birthday present in Berlin. That's the trick they played, they got you by the balls and they squeezed. Hard.

DAVID: Major, I simply can't see how this line of questioning –

ARNOLD: (*Turning on him*) David, what is this? What are you all of a sudden, Counsel for the Defense? What you want me to say? Objection overruled? Objection sustained? My line of questioning is establishing motive, Counsellor, plain, ordinary human motive. Why did he stay? Why did he play for them? Why was he the flag carrier for the regime? Why was he their servant? Not art or culture or music and its mystical power, but good old-fashioned insecurity, fear and jealousy. And that was only part of his reason for staying –

FURTWÄNGLER: (*Suddenly interrupting, blurting out*) Of course there was a conspiracy against me, a campaign. They controlled the press. Every word that was written, every word that was published. When I resigned from the Philharmonic, when I refused to take part in a film they made about the orchestra, oh, countless things of that kind, refusing to co-operate in one way or another, they were determined to keep me in my place. You mentioned the critic, Edwin von der Nüll. His praise of – of – that man may have been genuine, I have no idea. But his remarks were encouraged and guided, and then seized on.

They wanted another 'star', as they called it, to take my place. They had their own concert agency under a man called Rudolf Vedder, a human being beneath contempt. He was determined to foist K on the public. I'm not going to recount the difficulties I had with that man but if I tell you that his chief ally in this was Ludolf von Alvensleben, personal adjutant to Heinrich Himmler, and when that particular individual did not get his way he threatened only one sanction: death. They controlled every aspect of our lives. They manipulated, bullied and imposed their monstrous will. When they finally understood that I would do everything in my power to prevent art from being directed and supervised, they determined to undermine me. They regarded any action of dissent, however small, as a criticism of the state, tantamount to high treason.

ARNOLD: And you didn't have von der Nüll conscripted because of that review he wrote?

FURTWÄNGLER: (*Blazing*) I've told you, it's absolute nonsense. How could I have managed such a thing? He was in their power, not mine. It's a total lie. And I have never in my life tried or even wanted to silence my critics, never. I believe serious criticism to be an essential part of cultural life.
(*Turning to* DAVID; *becoming excited.*)
And the reason you have detected a certain distaste I have for K is not because I was jealous or insecure but because I have serious criticism to make of him. In my opinion, he is an intellectual conductor. He does not experience the piece afresh each time. He conducts only what he knows and wants, in other words the nuances, which is why the nuances are all exaggerated. The slow tempi are too slow, the fast ones too fast. The whole effect is somewhat hysterical – (*He falls silent.*)

ARNOLD: Wilhelm, I'm trying to understand you, I really am, believe me. You see, when you talk about cultural life, I'm lost. Because I am, to put it at its best, totally uncultured. So when I look at you, I don't see the great artist, the greatest conductor alive, I see a man, an ordinary guy, like a million other ordinary guys. And I ask myself, what keeps

him in a situation which he says he did everything in his
power to resist, except get the hell out of it? What keeps
him here, I ask myself? Not being a cultured guy, I don't
buy all this stuff about music preserving liberty, justice and
humanity. I look for ordinary reasons, reasons I can
understand, reasons my buddies can understand. So, if I
said to my buddies, imagine you love your wife – well,
maybe I'm stretching reality here – no, stay with me – I say
to them, imagine you love your wife and they tell you
you're being sent overseas. But they exempt some young
guy who it's possible could take your wife's fancy. What
would you do? Like a man they'd say, Steve, we'd do
everything we could to stay put. See, Wilhelm, I'm talking
about ordinary, everyday motives. Which is why I want to
discuss your private life.

DAVID: Oh, come along, Major, this can't be right –

ARNOLD: (*Quietly*) Objection overruled, Counsellor. I'm
establishing motive.

(*To* FURTWÄNGLER.)

How many illegitimate children do you have?

DAVID: Major, this is outrageous, what has this to do with
anything at all?

ARNOLD: You'll see. Wilhelm, did you hear the question?

FURTWÄNGLER: (*Barely audible*) I have illegitimate children –

ARNOLD: What?

FURTWÄNGLER: I said I have illegitimate children. I don't know
how many.

ARNOLD: No, I bet you don't. Four, five, six?

(*No response.*)

You like the ladies, don't you, Wilhelm?

(*No response.*)

Isn't it true that before every concert you got a woman in
your dressing room and gave her the old conductor's baton,
isn't that true?

DAVID: Major, this is deeply offensive and repugnant –

ARNOLD: You bet –

DAVID: – and totally irrelevant.

ARNOLD: Not so, Counsellor. The women threw themselves at

51

you, didn't they, Wilhelm? That secretary of yours, Berta Geissmar, who's now working for *Sir* Thomas Beecham, she wasn't only your secretary, she was your procuress, wasn't she? She procured women for you, didn't she, as many and as often as you wanted –

FURTWÄNGLER: Stop this, please, stop this –

ARNOLD: No, I'm not going to stop it, because if I said to my buddies, you're living in a whorehouse where you get the whores free, you going to leave? See, Wilhelm, I think you stayed because you were in paradise here. Adolf himself offered you a beautiful house and a special bomb shelter –

FURTWÄNGLER: I absolutely refused the house and the bomb shelter –

ARNOLD: But you see what I'm getting at? You didn't stay because you felt an affinity with your people, or because you wanted to preserve the traditions of which, I think you said, you were a guardian, or because you believed that art and music and culture were above politics. See, if I said to my buddies, you're top dog in your profession, favourite of the number one man in the country, you get all the women you lust after, you're highly paid, you get a gorgeous house and a personal, private bomb shelter if you want it, what you going to do, leave or stay? One voice comes back at me: *stay!*

DAVID: That's not a good argument, Major. If Dr Furtwängler did indeed enjoy all these – these privileges, he enjoyed them because of who he is and what he is –

ARNOLD: Now we're back to the great artist –

DAVID: Right. His position would have guaranteed him anything he wanted wherever he chose to live and work. That's true of any leading artist in any country in the world. They're rare specimens, Major, and that sets them apart –

ARNOLD: Okay, but it doesn't make them saints. They still have to get up and piss in the middle of the night, don't they? And they can be envious and vindictive and mean just like you and me. Well, just like me. Can't they?

(*No response.*)

See, Wilhelm, everybody says what a great benefactor you were to the Jews, but what about that Italian conductor?

FURTWÄNGLER: I don't understand what you're talking about, but if you're now referring to Arturo Toscanini, he is not a Jew, of course, but he is greatly loved by you Americans –

ARNOLD: No, I was thinking of another Italian –

FURTWÄNGLER: (*Not hearing* ARNOLD; *again addressing* DAVID, *rather over-excitedly*) – and to my taste, he is too disciplined, his tempi are too strict. If he were a greater artist, if he had deeper insights, a livelier imagination, greater warmth and devotion to the work, he would not have become so disciplined. This is why his success is disastrous. Inspiration and understanding in art are more important than discipline and autocratic behaviour.

ARNOLD: But otherwise you like the guy. (*He chuckles.*) I'm beginning to get the picture. You're not crazy about any of your rivals, are you? I guess it was the same with this other Italian, the one I was thinking of, de Sabata –

FURTWÄNGLER: De Sabata?

ARNOLD: Vittorio de Sabata. I have a letter here, written in 1939, which states: (*Reading.*) 'What should I do when Dr Furtwängler said to me that it was a piece of impudence for that Jew de Sabata to conduct Brahms. Since the day when de Sabata performed *Tristan* in Bayreuth, Furtwängler speaks only of "Jew Sabata".'

FURTWÄNGLER: Who wrote that letter?

ARNOLD: I'm not at liberty to tell you that. But it's a genuine letter. David, you have a copy in the file, it's a genuine letter.

FURTWÄNGLER: There's only one thing I can say. I have never said anything that goes counter to my convictions and simply cannot have said anything that did. Of course there were instances when I was speaking to specific Party members. I had to use their language, one had to say Heil Hitler, for example, but quite apart from these instances, I did not make any compromises by saying things other than I believed. And I have always been frank in my attitude towards the Jews –

ARNOLD: I believe that. But just answer the question, don't give me explanations –

FURTWÄNGLER: But I have to explain. An attitude must exist in one to make such an outburst possible. And this is what I deny. I know that even in the greatest anger I couldn't have said such a thing. De Sabata was my friend, one of my few close friends. I invited him to conduct my orchestra. We discussed his programme, we discussed everything –

ARNOLD: Okay, so, here's another letter, July 4, 1933, written by you to the Minister of Culture, Bernhard Rust. It's about this modern composer, a Jew, Arnold Schönberg who was about to be suspended. There's a copy of this one, too, in your file, David. This is what you wrote, Wilhelm. (*Reading.*) 'Arnold Schönberg is considered by the Jewish International as the most significant musician of the present. It must be recommended that he not be made a martyr.' What do you say to that?

FURTWÄNGLER: I say exactly what I said before. You have to use their language –

DAVID: And you didn't finish the letter, Major. (*Reading.*) 'And if he is suspended now – and I would not indeed consider this right – the question of indemnity should be treated with generosity.' He's pleading for the man, not condemning him –

ARNOLD: Then what about these things he said? 'Jewish pen-pushers should be removed from the Jewish press', 'Jewish musicians lack a genuine affinity with *our* music', and 'Jewish musicians are good businessmen with few scruples, lacking roots.' You deny you said these things?

FURTWÄNGLER: But it depends on the circumstances, to whom one was speaking, these attitudes simply don't exist in me, I used their language, of course I did, everyone did.

DAVID: Major, you have to balance those things – if indeed he said them – against his assistance to his Jewish colleagues. Listen to this, Major, from the transcript of the proceedings at Nürnberg –

ARNOLD: (*Enjoying this*) Okay, Counsellor, here we go, it's your day in court. But be careful, there's nothing I enjoy more than a guy putting his own neck in the noose.

DAVID: A Swedish businessman, Birger Dahlerus, testified in cross-examination that he had several meetings with

Hermann Göring. 'I first saw Göring', Dahlerus testified,
'embroiled in a stormy interview with Wilhelm
Furtwängler, the famous conductor of the Berlin
Philharmonic, who was vainly seeking permission to keep
his Jewish concert master.'

FURTWÄNGLER: Yes, I remember well, I was pleading for
Szymon Goldberg, a wonderful musician and a wonderful
man, the youngest Konzertmeister the orchestra ever had.
Thank God he escaped, and I pray that he is safe now –

ARNOLD: Why is it, Wilhelm, that everything you say touches
me so deeply?

DAVID: (*Flaring*) Emmi, read one of those letters to Mrs Sachs.
Pick any one, read it –

(EMMI, *uncertain, looks at* ARNOLD, *who, indifferent, gestures
for her to do as she's been told. She selects a letter at random.*)

EMMI: I can't decipher this signature, but – (*Reading.*) 'Please
remember that helping Jews was a capital offence. People
were being publicly hanged on mere suspicion of such
activities but Dr Furtwängler helped anyone who asked
him. I personally testify to having seen literally hundreds of
people lined up outside his dressing room after concerts to
ask for his help. He never turned anyone away. He gave me
money because I was unable to feed myself or my family
and then he helped me to escape to Sweden. He helped
countless people in similar ways.'

DAVID: Doesn't sound like much of an anti-Semite to me,
Major. These are acts of enormous courage –

ARNOLD: (*Smiling*) You don't listen to what I say, David. How
many times have I got to tell you I was in insurance? You
think I can't smell a phoney policy when it's shoved under
my nose? Sure, he helped Jews but that was just insurance,
his cover, because the whole time he was maestro of all he
surveyed. (*Turning to* FURTWÄNGLER.) See, Wilhelm, I
think you're cunning, devious, dealing off the bottom of the
pack. You were their boy, their creature. That's the case
against you, old pal. You were like an advertising slogan for
them. This is what we produce, the greatest conductor in
the world. And you went along with it. You may not have

been a member of the Party because the truth is, Wilhelm, you didn't need to be.

(*To* EMMI.)

Emmi, put that record on –

(EMMI *puts on the record of the Adagio from Bruckner's Seventh Symphony.*)

ARNOLD: You know what that is?

FURTWÄNGLER: Of course I know what that is –

ARNOLD: Okay, so what is it?

FURTWÄNGLER: The Seventh Symphony of Anton Bruckner. The Adagio.

ARNOLD: Who's conducting?

FURTWÄNGLER: I am.

ARNOLD: You know the last time it was played on these air waves?

FURTWÄNGLER: How should I know such a thing?

ARNOLD: Well then, I'll tell you. The last time this music was played on these air waves was after they announced that your pal Adolf had blown his brains out. Listen to it.

(*They listen.*)

Did they pick little K's recording? Did they pick some other band leader? No, they picked you and why? Because you and nobody else represented them so beautifully. When the Devil died they wanted his band leader to play the funeral march. (*He takes off the record.*) You were *everything* to them.

FURTWÄNGLER: I have always tried – I have tried to analyze myself closely. You are right, Major. I am no better than anybody else. But I must always say what my instincts are. In staying here, I believed – I thought – I walked a tightrope between exile and the gallows. You seem to be blaming me for not having allowed myself to be hanged.

I tried to defend the intellectual life of my people against an evil ideology. I did not directly oppose the Party because, I told myself, this was not my job. I would have benefitted no one by active resistance. But I never hid my opinions. As an artist I was determined that music, at least, would remain untouched, untainted. If I had taken any active part in politics I couldn't have remained here. Please understand me correctly: an artist cannot be entirely apolitical. He must have some political convictions because he is, after all, a human being. As a citizen, it is an artist's duty to express these convictions. But as a musician, I am more than a citizen. I am a citizen of this country in that eternal sense to which the genius of great music testifies. I know that a single performance of a great masterpiece was a stronger and more vital negation of the spirit of Buchenwald and Auschwitz than words. Human beings are free wherever Wagner and Beethoven are played. Music transported them to regions where the torturers and murderers could do them no harm.

(ARNOLD *grabs the baton from his desk, stands trembling before* FURTWÄNGLER, *and snaps it in half.* EMMI *puts her fingers in her ears.*)

ARNOLD: (*His rage erupting with quiet, terrifying menace*) Have you ever smelled burning flesh? I smelt it four miles away. Four miles away, I smelt it. I smell it now, I smell it at night because I can't sleep any more with the stench of it in my nostrils. I'll smell it for the rest of my life. Have you seen the crematoria and the gas ovens? Have you seen the mounds of rotting corpses being shovelled into gigantic craters by the men and women who murdered them? I saw these things with my own eyes. And I've seen it every night since, night after night, and I wake screaming seeing it. I know I won't sleep undisturbed ever again. You talk to me about culture and art and music? You putting that in the scales, Wilhelm? You setting culture and art and music against the millions put to death by your pals? The pals you could call to save a couple of Jews when thousands, millions of them, were being annihilated? Is that what you're putting on the scales? Yes, I blame you for not getting hanged, I blame you for your cowardice. You strutted and swaggered, king-pin in a shithouse. You talk to me of walking a tightrope between exile and the gallows, and I say to you, lies –

FURTWÄNGLER: (*Breaking down*) I love my country, I believe in art, what was I to do?

ARNOLD: Act courageously. Just think of real courage, think of what men like Emmi's father did, risking their lives, not their careers –
(*He sees* EMMI *has her fingers in her ears, yells at her.*)
For Chrissake, Emmi, take your goddam fingers out of your ears –
(*She does so, tense, strained.*)
I'm talking about your father, I'm talking about real courage, I'm talking about him risking his fucking life –
(*She screams, the chilling sound of one who can take no more. All stare at her, shocked.*)

EMMI: My father only joined the plot when he realized we could not win the war.

FURTWÄNGLER: Major, what kind of a world do you want? What kind of world are you going to make? Don't you honestly understand the power of art to communicate beauty and pain and triumph? Even if you can't admit it, don't you believe that music especially transcends language and national barriers and speaks directly to the human spirit? If you honestly believe the only reality is the physical world, you will have nothing left but feculence more foul-smelling than that which pervades your nights – (*Near to breakdown.*) This isn't just, this isn't fair. How was I to know what they were capable of? No one knew. No one knew they were gangsters, atrocious, depraved. (*He breaks down, buries his face in his hands.*) Oh God, I don't want to stay in this country. Yes, yes, it would have been better if I'd left in 1934, it would have been better if I'd left – (*He suddenly wretches.* EMMI *goes to him.*)

ARNOLD: (*Yelling*) Helmuth!
(RODE *comes to the door.*)
Show your friend to the toilet and then tell him to get the hell out of here.
(RODE *and* EMMI *help* FURTWÄNGLER.)
Emmi, Helmuth can manage –
(EMMI *ignores him and exits with* RODE *and* FURTWÄNGLER. ARNOLD *marches to the telephone table, sits, lifts the receiver and dials.*)

DAVID: You know what, Major? We'll never understand. Only tyrannies understand the power of art. I wonder how I would have behaved in his position? I'm not certain I'd have 'acted courageously'. And what about you, Major? I have a feeling we might just have followed orders.

ARNOLD: I'm only a claims assessor. Who cares about me? But everyone kept telling me your man was something special. And you know what? He's not special at all.

DAVID: You know what I say he is, Major?

ARNOLD: No, what do you say he is, David?

DAVID: I say he's like a fallen priest –

ARNOLD: (*Into telephone*) Alex Vogel. (*To* DAVID.) And what would you know about priests, Lieutenant Vile?

DAVID: (*A smile*) Only what I read in books.

ARNOLD: Yeah, and what did you read?

DAVID: That they can be inadequate human beings. They can lie, they can fornicate, they can drink, they can deceive. But they can still put God into the mouths of the faithful. If you believe in that sort of thing.

(DAVID *goes to the record player, removes the Bruckner, finds another record.*)

ARNOLD: You know what I say *you* are, David?

DAVID: I know what you say I am, Major.

ARNOLD: Yeah, but you're worse. You're a liberal piece of shit. You don't know right from wrong.

(EMMI *returns, slightly dazed, holding a visitor's card.*)

EMMI (*To* DAVID; *quietly*) He thanked me and gave me his visiting card.

(DAVID *half smiles, puts the other record on the turntable.*)

ARNOLD: (*Into the telephone*) Vogel? Arnold. I don't know if we've got a case that'll stand up, but we can sure as hell give him a hard time –

(*At full volume the sound of the subdued opening of Beethoven's Ninth Symphony.*)

ARNOLD: (*To* DAVID) Hey, turn that off, can't you see I'm on the phone? (*Into the telephone.*) Yeah, yeah, but it makes no – never mind, we got a tame journalist who'll write what we'll tell him. (*Listens.*) Yeah, a guy called Delbert Clark, *New York Times* –

(*The great chords sound.*)

ARNOLD: Jesus Christ, what the hell are you doing? Turn that goddam thing down –

(*But* DAVID *ignores him, sits, implacable, listening.* FURTWÄNGLER *stumbles into the bomb rubble, as if a broken man struggling to regain his composure.*)

ARNOLD: Turn it off!

(*In the rubble,* FURTWÄNGLER *hears the music but he cannot identify its source. His left hand trembles but it is only his way of sensing the tempo.*

After a while the music and the lights begin to fade to Blackout.)